THE FAMILY

Thomas Alexander

The Family by Thomas Alexander

Direct Light Publications
45 Dudley Court, Endell Street, London, WC2H 9RF

Permissions may be sought directly from Publishing Rights Department 45 Dudley Court, Endell Street, London, WC2H 9RF
Library of Congress Cataloguing in Publication Data
Application submitted.
British Library Cataloguing in Publication Data
Application submitted.
03 04 05 06 07 08 10 9 8 7 6 5 4 3

–

Edited by Shirin Laghai for Direct Light Publications.

Cover Design by SimplyA

Cover Photograph by Shirin Laghai

DIRECT
LIGHT

The Family

SYNOPSIS

Today, for the first time in longer than anyone can remember, the family are gathering. All of them. They are gathering to celebrate the engagement of the maternal niece, they are gathering to celebrate the last birthday of the patriarch, they are gathering to welcome home the prodigal son and his beautiful girlfriend.

They are going to celebrate all this with a slideshow.

But this is a family with secrets. A family that believes in sweeping things under the carpet. Of keeping things in the family. Of staying together no matter what the cost.

This is a family that believes in taking photographs.

Candid photographs.

Photographs of things no one thought anyone else knew about.

Photographs of each and every dark and secret moment they have kept hidden.

Photographs of people when no one else was there.

Photos that deal with the remnants of child abuse, infidelity, loss, destruction, and missed birthday parties.

It's all coming out today. In black and white. On slides for everyone to see.

It's all coming out tonight and everyone's going to know everything. No one's sleeping, and when it's over, there may not even be a family left.

ABOUT THE AUTHOR

Thomas Alexander has worked in almost all forms of theatre, from opera to children's performances, working as everything from stage hand to costume designer, and has seen his work translated into four different languages and performed as far afield as America and Afghanistan.

His complete plays, along with his first novel, *A Scattering Of Orphans,* have been published by Direct Light Publications.

Also by the Author

PLAYS

Happiness
Murder Me Gently
The Family
Begat
The Crossroads Country
Great
The Visitor
When Dusk Brings Glory
The Recruitment Officer
Writer's Block
The Last Christmas
Writing William
The Big Match

ONE ACT PLAYS

Four Widows and A Funeral
For Arts Sake
The TV
Life TM
The Dance
The Pink Cow

ADAPTATIONS

William Shakespeare's R3
Othello

NOVELS

A Scattering Of Orphans

FOREWORD

Several years ago I was sitting at the home of a friend with her then-teenage daughter watching a movie. We were watching a scene in an office set in the 1980's, and the daughter turned to me suddenly and asked: "What's that on his desk?"

I looked at the scene but I couldn't see anything out of place, apart from, perhaps, something unclear in the background which I'd taken to be nothing more than a prop telephone.

"What?" I said. "Behind the typewriter?"

The girl looked at the screen and nodded, satisfied.

"I always wondered what a typewriter looks like!"

There is, in the tech world, a term called transient technology. For everything that lasts a generation or more - like the microwave or the TV - there are just as many inventions that quickly fade out of use. The minidisc. The laserdisc. The pager. These are all things which survived no longer than a decade but which, for a time, were incredibly important to the consumer.

One of these transient technologies was the slide projector. If you were born at a certain time, before social media, before mobile phones and the internet, people used to share photos by buying a special kind of film for a camera (don't get me started on film for cameras!) called slide film. They'd then get these developed or, more correctly, mounted into little white plastic slide cases no more than a couple of inches wide which could, in turn, be put, one at a time, into a projector and you would invite your friends round to look at them, projected up on a screen in your living room.

This form of social torture, common amongst certain types of friends in the seventies and eighties, would be accentuated by the fact that each slide had to be manually inserted the right way up, in the right manner, and with the right focus for anything to be recognisable at all.

If you were cool - and boy, were we not cool - these slides could be placed one by one with painstaking care into a carousel which allowed for automatic feeding. This level of care was necessary not only because if they were the wrong way round your friends would laugh at you, but also because every so often the damn thing would jam, and would often take an hour with a fork and a death-wish to rectify, during which time your guests, nee prisoners, would have to make small talk while they cheered you on, all the while secretly hoping that the damn thing was beyond repair and they would be spared the four hundred and five photos of your Auntie Gladys' birthday party from the year before – which they were all at anyway.

Trust me. If your friends posting photos of their lunch online annoys you, imagine sitting in a room with them while they went back through their entire diet for the past year.

The thing is, for all the negative things there are to say about transient technology, there is also a wistfulness that goes with it. A nostalgia that nothing else quite manages to emulate.

Microwaves and mobile phones have changed drastically over the years, as have Walkmans and computers. But all these technologies have evolved, and evolved at their own rate. You could have had an iPhone for almost ten years now, and while technology-wise the first one is a quantum leap behind the current one on sale, it's only six grams heavier. Your TV may now be able to connect to the internet, be touchscreen, and wafer thin, but it still occupies the same spot in your house that it always did and broadcasts many of the same programs.

Transient technologies, however, have none of these drawbacks. They existed for a time during a period of your life and then… disappeared. Tapes. Minidiscs. Even, perhaps, records. They all occupy an area of your history and connect you to those times that, say, a mobile phone cannot.

Whether you remember trying to jog with a CD Walkman while balancing it and cursing its capability to whirr at you, or whether you remember losing your first novel because you were writing it on an electronic word processor which wiped everything on the disc during a power outage – as has happened to me – there is something about the nostalgia it gives you that is very hard to replicate.

With slides it was the sound they made. The clack-clack as one slide was ejected and another took its place. The hum of the fan as it cooled the one hundred watt lens that cost a fortune to replace.

For me those sounds are family. They are the sounds of family and friends arguing over what they are looking at and whether they have ever been there. They are the sounds of people who are in a room for no other reason than love and the lack of an excuse not to be there. They are the past. Markers in your evolution from what we were to what we are today.

And like all pasts, they are best left there.

The slide projector takes a fairly prominent place in The Family, due as much to theatricality as nostalgia. If you haven't seen one before, go and watch some old films with scenes where lectures take place. Visit an old college with professors who have never been able to move on. Or, if you don't feel like moving, simply wait. It's only a matter of time before slide projectors become retro again and replace social media once more.

Thomas Alexander – 2014

AUTHOR'S NOTE

Due to the nature of the play, the ages of the cast, with the exception of GRANDMA, is largely irrelevant. However, while I would recommend directors take licence with this, the generation gaps should be at least plausable so as not to spoil the denouement, even if the audiences believe that it's a directorial choice. Again, this does not apply to the character of GRANDMA, whose age is listed below.

A number of models need to be used for the **SLIDES** *including the character of LIZ who does not appear in the production, and the family dog who does.*

The Family

CAST

No of cast: 10

MUM (Kim)

DAD (Daniel)

KYLE   First born.

MARTY   (Martin) Second born.

DAVID   Family friend.

GRANDMA Twenties. Pretty. Similarity to MUM

BOB   Older brother to MUM.

SARAH   Daughter of BOB. Cousin to
MARTY and KYLE.

JOSIE   Girlfriend of MARTY.

EMILY   Younger sister to MARTY and KYLE.

THE FAMILY

ACT I

ACT 1

WE OPEN ON A LARGE LIVING ROOM.

AT STAGE RIGHT STANDS A FRONT DOOR LEADING OUT ONTO A DRIVEWAY. STAGE LEFT, PATIO DOORS LEAD TO A REAR GARDEN.

A LARGE COUCH AND MATCHING ARMCHAIRS SIT CENTRE DOWNSTAGE LOOKING OUT AT THE AUDIENCE. A SLIDE PROJECTOR, IN FRONT OF THEM, POINTS OUT INTO THE AUDIENCE.

UPSTAGE RIGHT THE STAIRS RUN UP AND OFF WHILE A DOORWAY AND AN OPEN WINDOW DIVIDER LEAD INTO A KITCHEN BEYOND, A REFRIGERATOR CLEARLY VISIBLE

NOTE: HOWEVER THIS UPSTAGE AREA IS STAGED IT MUST ALLOW FOR A LARGE WHITE AREA BEHIND THE ACTORS FOR THE SLIDE PROJECTIONS WHICH, WHILE THE CAMERA POINTS OUTWARDS, ARE ALWAYS PROJECTED BEHIND THEM.

KYLE ENTERS AND SITS CENTRE WEARILY ONTO THE COUCH.

REACHING ACROSS HE TURNS ON THE PROJECTOR, CASTING A GLOW ONTO THE BACK WALL.

HE STARES OUT FOR A MINUTE, DEJECTED, THEN STARTS TO TEAR UP.

ANGRY WITH HIMSELF HE WIPES HIS EYES, TURNS OFF THE PROJECTOR, AND PULLS OUT A PIECE OF PAPER FROM HIS POCKET AND READS, PRACTICING HIS SPEECH.

KYLE   (STIFFLY) Ladies and gentlemen. (BEAT) No, shit. Fuck. Can't even get that right. (HE PULLS A PEN OUT OF ANOTHER POCKET AND CROSSES IT OUT ANGRILY, WRITING) Family (BEAT) and friends. It's not often we get everyone together like this so I won't take long. I just wanna say congratulation to Sarah (HE IS NOT AT EASE) for her upcoming wedding and… (HE CRUMPLES UP THE PAPER, ANGRY AND BITTERLY UNHAPPY) Fuck.

HE PULLS OUT ANOTHER PIECE OF PAPER AND STARTS WRITING ON THAT.

KYLE   (CONT.) Motherfuckers…

A DOORBELL RINGS.

KYLE   Hang on!

HE GOES OVER TO THE DOOR AND OPENS IT. MARTY AND JOSIE STAND ON THE OTHER SIDE.

MARTY   Hey…

KYLE   (REACHING OUT AND HUGGING HIM) My man!

MARTY   (UNCOMFORTABLE WITH THE STRENGTH OF THE HUG) Yeah, alright. What is this, gay night?

KYLE   Thought you weren't getting in til tomorrow?

MARTY   Is the car alright there? Whose're all the cars in the driveway?

KYLE   We thought you were getting here in the morning.

MARTY   We thought we'd get here early.

KYLE   And who's the lovely lady?

JOSIE   Hi.

MARTY   Josie, this is my brother Kyle…

JOSIE   Nice to meet you.

KYLE   Where'd you find this one then!

MARTY   What's with all the cars?

KYLE   We got started early. You know, with the wedding and everything. They're in the garden. (GESTURING TO THE BAGS JOSIE'S HOLDING) Let me take that.

MARTY PUTS THE BAGS ON THE FLOOR AND WALKS INTO THE ROOM.

MARTY   Emily here?

KYLE   Emily?

MARTY   She here?

KYLE   (TO JOSIE) Emily's our sister. (TO MARTY)
Not yet.

MARTY   This place hasn't changed at all.

JOSIE   (TO MARTY AS HE TAKES HER BAG)
Thank you.

MARTY   Look at it! Josie, seriously, it hasn't…

KYLE   (TO JOSIE) You're American?

MARTY   I thought they'd knocked that wall through.

JOSIE   Illinois. Yes.

MARTY   It's exactly the same as I remember it!

KYLE   Our mother's American? He tell you that?

MARTY   Like when we were kids.

JOSIE   He mentioned that, yeah.

KYLE   This is where, god, I remember this, I was, what two? No, must have been older than that. It was bath night. Bath night was Saturday night. Every Saturday, six o'clock. Did we used to have one in the week? I can't remember. Probably not.

Just face and hands in the week. But Saturday. Any time of the year. Bath night. Anyway, this is where it happened. Not here, of course, there was… We had a fire here. A real old coal fire. I used to have to poke it every morning. That was my job. This was, what, only twenty years ago and we had a coal fire! Anyway; we'd come in here, in the winter and, it was freezing, you know, coming out of the bath, by the time we finished, but anyway we'd come in here and try to get as close to the fire as we could. Fight for it. Who could warm up faster while we watched some American programs on the TV. Come in here, fight for the fire. (BEAT) And Kyle here sat on it. Just sat on it. I can't remember why. Not an open fire, of course, one of those closed off metal frames, but he just came in, towel round his neck and sat on it. Right here.

KYLE   Trust you to remember that.

JOSIE   Were you alright?

MARTY   Same thing with my arm. That happened today and you'd have social services round in an instant. There's no way in this day and age they'd believe that a, what, eight year old would simply sit on a fire to keep warm, which, I promise, is exactly what he did, but these days, they'd have you in for observation and the rest of us in a home.

JOSIE   What happened to your arm?

KYLE   He broke it jumping out of the upstairs window with a bed sheet tied round his neck.

MARTY   I must have lied to Mum or something because she didn't take me to the hospital for a week. When they asked her when it happened she simply said; yesterday. (BEAT) It hasn't changed a bit.

KYLE   What did you expect?

MARTY   I don't know. I mean. Childhood homes are always smaller, aren't they?

A PAIR OF YOUNG CHILDREN, KYLE AND MARTY –

AGED AROUND TEN – RUN THROUGH THE ROOM, CHASING EACH OTHER, LAUGHING. COMPLETELY UNSEEN BY THE GROWN UPS, THEY EXIT AGAIN.

MARTY   (CONT.) Nothing's as big as when you're little. (BEAT) But, I don't know, the wallpaper? You have thought they'd have changed that.

KYLE   So, little brother. How's the big city?

MARTY   Mum and Dad are out the back?

KYLE   They're talking with David.

MARTY   Yeah?

KYLE   Uncle Bob's there.

MARTY   Bob?

KYLE   Sarah's with him.

MARTY   Really? She must be, what?

KYLE   Getting married.

MARTY   Really?!

KYLE   Some guy from college.

MARTY   Wow.

JOSIE   Martin?

MARTY   Right. Sorry. Through there, up to the left.

EXIT JOSIE.

MARTY   (CONT.) Married? Jesus.

KYLE   Yeah. I know. Got to say, it's not what I expected, you know? Not what I expected at all.

MARTY   I didn't even know… college?

KYLE   She didn't go. I didn't mean she went. He went. You know. She's working at that café and I mean, you know, I haven't really gone into the details, the only thing I know is

Dad's all chuffed because the boy went to college and Bob...

MARTY   Shit. Yeah. Bob.

KYLE   It's not what I expected, you know?

MARTY   Well, you know. Good for the girl.

KYLE   Yeah?

MARTY   Gets her out from under him, I suppose. What they all doing here? I thought the thing was tomorrow.

KYLE   Started early, I guess. How was the drive, long?

MARTY   Something like that, yeah.

KYLE   So. (BEAT) How's, you know, everything?

MARTY   Good.

KYLE   You still writing?

MARTY   It's my job, Kyle. Yeah, I'm writing. It's what I do.

KYLE   Just asking. (PAUSE) You know, you don't want to bring it up or anything but I think Dad was reading one of your early ones.

MARTY   Yeah? Which one?

KYLE   The one about, you know.

MARTY   Blue Rainbow?

KYLE   Mum found it in the upstairs toilet and it wasn't me, so...

MARTY   You're living here?

KYLE   Well, you know, temporary like.

MARTY   What happened to the flat?

KYLE   Nothing 'happened'! It's just...

MARTY   How old are you?

KYLE   They need me, I mean, Dad's, you know…

MARTY   Dad's fine.

KYLE   How would you know?

MARTY   We talk.

KYLE   He's not fine. He can barely hear…

MARTY   I thought he'd got a hearing aid?

KYLE   And he forgets things.

MARTY   We all forget things. Give me a man over forty and I'll give you a jigsaw with pieces missing.

KYLE   That one of your books?

MARTY   Not yet, no.

KYLE   He forgets things.

MARTY   You're twenty-eight years old, Kyle. It's time you took responsibility for yourself.

KYLE   I'm thirty-three, Marty. Maybe it's not only Dad, yeah?

MARTY   All I'm saying is. It's not good for you. Living here. It's not healthy. Kim…

KYLE   You heard from her?

MARTY   Kim's moved on with her life. It's time you did too, you know? Listen. Come to the city…

KYLE   Don't worry about it.

MARTY   Come to the city. We'll find you a little place.

KYLE   I'm fine!

MARTY   Or get a place in town. It's not going to cost much and…

KYLE   (ANGRILY) You know, when I need a hand from my little brother I'll ask for one, you know what I mean?

Shit, you've only been here a few minutes and already you're in at me. Fuck off back to the city. It's not like we need you here anyway.

MARTY	Yeah.
KYLE	Just…
MARTY	Don't worry about it.
PAUSE.	
MARTY	What's with the projector?
KYLE	It's a projector. Slides.
MARTY	I haven't seen one of these for…
KYLE	Dad's gonna use it tonight.
MARTY	You're kidding!
KYLE	Yeah.
MARTY	Oh, god. He's going to pull out the baby shit?
KYLE	You brought your girlfriend. What do you think?
MARTY	Shit.
KYLE	And you may want to watch that language as well.
MARTY	What did I say?
KYLE	Shit.
MARTY	Jesus. (HE GOES TO THE DOOR) You say Bob's there?
KYLE	Yeah. He's… He's been around a lot recently.
MARTY	How old is she, anyway?
KYLE	I don't know. Twenty? Twenty-three.
ENTER JOSIE.	

MARTY   What's he like?

KYLE   Haven't met him.

MARTY   We're sure he's a guy?

JOSIE   Who's this?

KYLE   Our cousin's getting married.

JOSIE   She's gay?

KYLE   Well, she's happy about it, if that's what you mean.

MARTY   We were never sure.

KYLE   You think…

MARTY   Give them a call.

KYLE   Mum?

JOSIE   Your folks?

MARTY   They're in the garden.

KYLE   You give them a call.

MARTY   (GOING TO THE DOOR) Mum! (PAUSE) Mum!

KYLE   (TO JOSIE) How was the drive?

JOSIE   Good. Yeah. I mean, it's like, what have you guys got against M's.

MARTY   Who's that with them?

KYLE   Sorry?

JOSIE   You keep closing them. M1 – flooding. M4 – greenery.

MARTY   That David?

KYLE   I had this friend, I was driving back from London and he kept looking out the window once we're over the bridge and he's like: "where the fuck," sorry, "is toledai?"

JOSIE   Nice.

KYLE   And I'm like, what? And he says, like: "it keeps saying toledai, twenty miles, toledai, fifteen miles, toledai, one mile, toledai, forty-five miles."

JOSIE   Ha!

MARTY   David's here?

KYLE   He's in the garden, yeah.

MARTY   With Bob.

KYLE   In the garden. Anyway, the point is, like, that you know, toledai is the Welsh for toilet.

JOSIE   Your brother told me.

MARTY   You don't think that's strange?

KYLE   He's a friend. What do you want?

ENTER MUM.

MUM   Here he is!

MARTY   Mum.

MUM   Let me look at you. Ah, he's a handsome one. Look at that cheekbone.

MARTY   I owe it all to you!

MUM   (KISSING HIM) And don't you forget it. I thought you weren't getting in til tomorrow?

MARTY   And yet you start the party without me?

MUM   Now you watch that mouth around your father. You know how it gets him. Let me look at you. My son the big man. This boy, I tell you, he was the frailest thing...

MARTY   Mum.

MUM   Wouldn't know it now to look at him but he was the frailest thing. Break him with a twig you would. Break

him with a stiff wind we used to say. Now look at him! (PAUSE)
And who's this?

KYLE	Josie.
JOSIE	Hi. Josie.
MUM	You're American.
MARTY	She's from Wisconsin.
JOSIE	Redbrook.
MUM	Really? That's great!
JOSIE	You kept the accent.

MUM   It comes and goes. Comes and goes. I have no
idea why but if I'm cooking, anything in the kitchen, the whole
thing comes right back. Can't find anything Welsh in it. Dishes,
everything. But you put me in front of the telly, no matter what
the show, I'm Welsh all the way.

JOSIE   Well it sounds good anyway.

MUM   You're a sweet young thing. (TO KYLE) Get
your father in. (TO MARTY) We've only got the one room.

MARTY   That's fine.

MUM   (UNSURE) Well, whatever. How'd you kids
meet anyway?

JOSIE   I'm...

MARTY   She's my boss. Well, was anyway.

JOSIE   I handle the American arm of publishing for
Waterhouse.

MUM   I'm sorry?

MARTY   The... My publisher.

JOSIE   We're thinking about moving his books into
the market.

MUM   Is that right, now? Well, my son, the cross Atlantic divide!

MARTY   Well, there's still some stuff to be ironed out but...

MUM   Well, you're welcome, anyway. Like I said there's only the one bedroom but I suppose that's all you'll be wanting. You're always welcome.

MARTY   Don't worry about it, Mum.

MUM   Your father'll...

MARTY   Kyle was telling me...

MUM   He's fine.

KYLE   Mum!

MUM   He's fine!

KYLE   He's not fine!

MUM   How long you staying?

MARTY   Mum...

KYLE   You're welcome...

MARTY   What's Bob doing here?

THERE'S A DROP IN TEMPERATURE.

MUM   That how you talk to people, now?

MARTY   He shouldn't be here.

MUM   He's my brother.

MARTY   He shouldn't be here.

KYLE   Martin.

MUM   He's my brother.

MARTY   He's MY brother!

MUM   He's your uncle and...

JOSIE	I'd love to meet more of your family.

MUM   See. You're home! Let's leave it at that, shall we? He was always the one with the mouth. Even when he was a little kid. He had these big teeth, lots of them. Growing out of everywhere, they were, so it was difficult for him to get the words, you know, the shape of them. When he was little, I mean, really little, he couldn't say words with S's, you understand? Because of the teeth. So he used to make up new words, all on his own. Lots of them. You know what he used to say for spoon? Bunt. Couldn't say spoon, so he just called it a bunt. Right up to school. Had a devil of a job getting him out of it.

MARTY	Thanks, Mum.
JOSIE	No, that's so sweet. Say it for me?
MARTY	No!
JOSIE	Go on. What was it again?
MUM	Bunt.
JOSIE	Bunt! Say it.
MARTY	Bunt. I need a bunt for my soup.
JOSIE	That's classic. You should get that into the book.

ENTER DAD, BOB, DAVID, AND SARAH.

MUM	Look who's here.
DAD	Emily came?
MARTY	Hey Dad.
DAD	Oh, Martin.
MUM	This is Josie
DAD	Oh, yeah?
MUM	She's American.
JOSIE	It's a pleasure to meet you, sir.

DAD	Ha. No. Thanks. That's…
MUM	You can call us Dan and Kim, okay?
JOSIE	I'm sorry it's just where we're from…
MARTY	How was the garden?
DAD	We were going to have a look at some slides.
MUM	Daniel! Not now!
DAD	I found boxes of them. Boxes. You believe that? In the attic. Your mother was clearing out the attic again and…
MUM	They don't want to see any slides…
DAD	Just a few. Before dinner.
MUM	We just ate.
DAD	Just a few. While we got everyone here.
MARTY	I don't know, Dad, it's been a drive and…
DAD	We got champagne if you want it?
MUM	(TO JOSIE AND MARTY) Now, did you eat?

DAD HEADS OVER TO THE PROJECTOR. KYLE JOINS HIM, STEERING CLEAR OF THE OTHERS. MARTY AND JOSIE HANG IN THE BACKGROUND, UNCOMFORTABLE.

DAVID   Beer?

DAVID GOES INTO THE KITCHEN.

THE FOLLOWING DIALOGUE BUILDS TO A CACOPHONY IN TERMS OF SPEED AND RHYTHM.

MARTY	We ate in the car.
MUM	(TO JOSIE) How was the drive?
MARTY	Fine.

JOSIE   I was just telling Kyle...

MUM   I miss the accent. How long you been here?

JOSIE   A couple of years...

MARTY   Josie was doing her PhD.

MUM   PhD eh?

JOSIE   Nanotechnology.

MUM   Your Dad's got slides.

MARTY   We're not staying...

MUM   Of course you are, don't be silly. You are.

JOSIE   That's very kind...

DAD   You know how they get the bubbles?

KYLE   Grit.

DAD   Grit. Thing doesn't work without imperfection, don't you love that?

KYLE   The first bottles...

DAD   First bottles couldn't sell, see. Who wants wine with bubbles?

KYLE   Only England.

DAVID (OFF) Fridge?

DAD   England was the only importer.

MUM   We don't see enough of this one, do we Dad?

MARTY   There's a hotel...

DAD   Someone close the curtains!

MARTY   And I thought, maybe, just for the night.

MUM   The rooms made up. So you're staying. That's all there is to it.

KYLE   (TO JOSIE) I'm not kidding. Run.

DAD   I think I've got it to work.

MUM   (TO MARTY) Sit by your Dad.

KYLE   Seriously.

JOSIE   These going to be baby things?

KYLE   Photos.

MUM   (TO JOSIE) Aren't you wonderful.

DAVID   I can't find the champagne?

MUM   It's in the bottom.

BOB   I'll help you.

DAVID It's not in here!

MUM   It's in the bottom! Under the carrots.

BOB   We have glasses?

MUM   Top shelf, above the sink.

MARTY   Dad. (BEAT) You know how to work this?

DAD (NODDING HELLO) Put that in would you?

MARTY PLUGS IT IN.

DAVID Got it!

BOB   There's only four.

DAD   (SWITCHING ON THE THING) There we go.

MUM   There's plastic under the sink.

DAD   Is it on?

MARTY   This isn't going to be embarrassing, is it?

DAD   What's to embarrass?

MARTY Mum's already done the bunt story.

DAVID   Who's having champagne?

JOSIE   You must be Sarah?

SARAH Hi.

JOSIE   Martin tells me you're getting married married.

SARAH Next week. Yeah.

JOSIE   You must be excited.

SARAH I was going to wear white. I was thinking about… White is traditional, isn't it? That's what I think anyway. But is it only tradition if you always do it? Is that how it works?

JOSIE   I think it's whatever works for you

SARAH (NODS) But they don't allow black for weddings, do they. Though that would be more symbolic, wouldn't it? Black? The death of one family. But then, is it only symbolic if everyone understands it. Is that how it works?

MUM   (TO BOB) Put the glasses on the table.

DAD   It's your life.
BOB   Sarah.

SARAH THEN LEAVES TO HELP BOB WITH THE CHAMPAGNE.

MARTY   That's what I'm worried about.

JOSIE   Marty?

MARTY MOVES BACK TO JOSIE.

DAD   It was working before.

KYLE   (TO DAD) I think it's the other way round.

MUM   Champagne?

DAVID   You want me to help pour?

MUM   Who's for champagne?

DAD   (TO KYLE) Leave it alone!

MUM (TO DAVID) Sarah's helping Bob. You just sit there.

KYLE Who invented the slide projector anyway?

DAVID Okay.

DAD That's a good… (GETTING SOMEWHERE WITH THE PROJECTOR) Ah! That's a good question. No one knows, right? The Sturm Lantern was the first magic lantern, so I guess that was the first.

MUM David. Champagne.

JOSIE (TO MARTY) Is she alright?

KYLE Sarah? Yeah.

MARTY How you doing?

JOSIE I think she hates me.

MARTY She doesn't know you.

KYLE Don't take it personally.

MARTY This is what we meant. She's always like that.

JOSIE As long as it's not me.

MARTY It's not you.

JOSIE Your Mum's nice.

MARTY (WITHOUT CONVICTION) They're

DAVID Thank you.

KYLE When was that?

DAD 1676.

MUM Sarah, you sit there. Here's your cup.

DAVID (TO BOB) You've got to tip the glass.

MUM Father. Champagne!

KYLE (FIDDLING WITH THE PROJECTOR) Try that. What else happened?

MUM Father!

DAD I'll get it in a minute. New Pope. New Tsar as well, and then they start the Turkish war...

good people.

JOSIE Your Mum seems nice.

MARTY Just... just don't get her started on the champagne that's all I'm saying. Look, listen, if you'd rather go...

JOSIE No. It's just... She's thinking about getting married in black.

MARTY That sounds about right for her.

JOSIE In black!

MARTY Don't worry about it.

MUM Bob, here. Take his. Before the bubbles go. Martin!

KYLE Try that again. There was a war with Turkey?

MUM Martin...

DAVID Kim. Sit with me.

MUM Martin!

DAD Five years. It was the Ottoman empire of course. You know, there were sixteen wars between them. Sixteen! Last one was when your grandfather was a lad.

MARTY (TO JOSIE) Champagne?

KYLE Is that right?

JOSIE (SOTTO) Do you think there's something to eat?

DAD It'll bend if you do that. Give it me here!

MUM   Just take them. That everyone?

JOSIE   I haven't eaten since England.

KYLE   I've got it!

DAD   Give it to me!

MARTY   Mum, we got any snacks or anything?

KYLE   Try it!

MUM   Father!

DAD   Hang on.

KYLE   Try it!

GRANDMA ENTERS. A YOUNG, ATTRACTIVE WOMAN, SHE SITS AT THE BACK OF THE GROUP.

MUM   (TO DAD) Leave that to Kyle. Take this and get the kids something to eat!

DAD   Hold your horses.

KYLE   (TURNING IT ON) Move your fingers.

MUM   (BARKING) Daniel!

DAD   Hang…

A LIGHT FLARES UP OVER THE BACK WALL BEHIND THEM AS THE PROJECTOR STARTS UP. ALTHOUGH THE FAMILY ARE LOOKING OUT TOWARDS THE AUDIENCE AND THE PROJECTOR IS FACING DOWN STAGE THE PICTURE ITSELF IS UPSTAGE, PROJECTED AGAINST THE REAR WALL.

THE FAMILY FALL SILENT. THERE IS A CLACK AND THE FIRST SLIDE COMES UP.

THE CACOPHONY IS OVER. THE PAUSES ARE LONG, THE SENTENCES DELIBERATE AND CHOSEN.

_____**SLIDE**_____ A SLIDE OF A BOY ON A BIKE ON A BEACH, RIDING HARD INTO THE WIND, A KITE

FLYING BEHIND HIM.

MUM   Where's that?

KYLE   Is that me?

DAD   Morecambe. I think.

MARTY   This was before the Mars Bars

DAD   '83? '81?

MUM   It was the year we did the kitchen. I remember
the floors.

MARTY   Where was I?

DAVID   I had to wait in for the plumber. You gave me
keys.

MARTY   Really?

MUM   We'd given you the old Brownie, remember? It
had the…

MARTY   (OVERLAPPING) It had the negative
viewfinder.

MUM   You saw everything upside down.

KYLE   We stayed at that guesthouse behind the park.

MUM   Your father went missing…

MARTY   I remember something about porridge.

DAD   They wouldn't let you leave.

MUM   They gave you this huge bowl of porridge and
wouldn't let you leave until you'd eaten it.

MARTY   I'd forgotten that.

JOSIE   How old were you?

MARTY   I was… How old was I?

MUM   You'd have been eight, I think.

MARTY   I was eight.

KYLE   I remember the park.

MARTY   I just remember the porridge. They put salt on
it.

DAD   We done?

THERE IS A CLACK AND THE SLIDE CHANGES.

_____**SLIDE**_____ A CLOSE UP OF MUM, SAD.

CLACK AS THE SLIDE CHANGES.

_____**SLIDE**_____ THE CAR WRECK.

CLACK AS THE SLIDE CHANGES.

_____**SLIDE**_____ A HOUSE.

DAVID   Where's that?

MUM   I don't recognize...

DAVID   Who's that outside?

DAD   It's Scotland isn't it?

KYLE   Why do you say that?

DAD   I think that's Loch Lomond.

KYLE   How can you tell?

DAD   It's got the largest surface of the lochs.

MUM   It's probably in there by accident.

DAD   Twenty-seven miles.

MUM   Boots probably. Mixing it up.

DAD   I don't think we've been there though. I don't
think we can have been there.

JOSIE   You never went to Scotland?

DAD   I always meant to... I don't think we can have
been here!

MUM   It's probably by mistake. Someone else's slides got mixed up with ours. Turn it over.

DAD   I don't see how we can have been there?

MUM   Daniel!

GRANDMA   Kim.

MUM   Daniel!

HE STARTS, AS IF COMING BACK FROM A THOUGHT AND CLICKS THE SWITCH.

CLACK AS THE SLIDE CHANGES.

_____**SLIDE**_____ A BABY PHOTO. MARTY.

JOSIE   Aww!

MARTY   Oh, god. This is what I was afraid of.

JOSIE   (TO MUM) How old is he there?

MUM   Ten months.

JOSIE   What's he got in his hand?

MUM   That would be…

DAVID   Shit, by the looks of it.

MUM   David!

DAVID   Sorry.

MUM   I should wash your mouth out with soap.

DAVID   Promises, promises.

JOSIE   You were such a cute little thing.

MUM   We'd just got you. And look at you, you're smiling at us already.

MARTY   Can we move on now?

JOSIE   How old was he when he came to you?

MARTY   Josie..!

DAD   Eight months. Eight months, two days.

THEY ARE ALL SURPRISED AT THIS. DAD, HUMBLED, FIDDLES WITH THE PROJECTOR.

DAD   There's a piece of something in here. I think that's why it keeps sticking.

MUM   He was ten months then, I think we'd taken him to…

CLACK AS THE SLIDE CHANGES.

_____**SLIDE**_____ A SCHOOL YARD. TEACHERS AND PUPILS LOOKING UP AT AN OPEN GATE, A TINY FIGURE FLEEING THROUGH IT, NOTHING MORE THAN A SHADOW IN THE MIX OF THE ANGRY TEACHERS AND PLAYING KIDS.

DAD   That's got it.

MUM   (FADING) …the doctor. (LOUD) Does anyone know what that is?

KYLE   New to me.

MARTY   That's Croisty's, right? We didn't go there.

MUM   Bob?

SARAH   I think… (THE ROOM TURNS AS ONE TO LOOK AT HER) I think that's where I went when I ran away from school.

THE ROOM TURNS BACK. UNCOMFORTABLE.

SARAH   I didn't like what they were doing with the mice. I didn't like what they were doing so I ran away. All the way. I ran home and hid in the shed at the bottom of the garden.

CLACK AS THE SIDE CHANGES.

PAUSE.

_____**SLIDE**_____ A DOG.

KYLE / MARTY   Barney!

MUM   Oh, not that mutt.

MARTY   (TO JOSIE) Barney was our first dog.

MUM   He was your only dog!

MARTY   Mum hated him.

MUM   Perfectly good clothes he'd rip up. For no good reason.

KYLE   He was bored.

MUM   He was a mutt!

JOSIE   What happened to him.

MUM   He ran away.

MARTY   He didn't run away!

MUM   How would you know?

KYLE   We always knew.

MARTY   Mum gave him to some people while we were at school.

MUM   How did you know that?

MARTY   Kyle saw them when he was bunking off school.

MUM   Kyle?

KYLE   I was in the shed in the garden.

MUM   I always thought you never knew.

KYLE   Martin was more upset with you than me.

MARTY   I don't think I ever forgave you, to be honest.

MUM   Martin!

CLACK AS THE SLIDE CHANGES.

_____**SLIDE**_____ CLOSE UP OF A TUBE OF

LIPSTICK, LYING ON A BED.

MARTY   I was a kid!

MUM   To say something like that.

MARTY   I was a kid. Don't worry about it.

JOSIE   Was that the dog in…

MARTY   Downtime. Yes.

JOSIE   I loved that part.

MUM   Still, to say something…

DAVID   Not to interrupt but does anyone actually know what that thing is?

MUM   I have no idea.

MARTY   Sarah?

SARAH SHAKES HER HEAD.

PAUSE.

MUM   Anyone?

CLACK AS THE SLIDE CHANGES.

_____**SLIDE**_____ A HAIR-CLIP, LYING ON A PILLOW, SMOKED AND SHADED IN MAPPLETHORPE STYLE.

DAVID   That's beautiful.

MUM   That's not mine.

KYLE   Anyone?

THE ROOM IS SILENT.

CLACK AS THE SLIDE CHANGES.

_____**SLIDE**_____ THE CAR WRECK.

CLACK AS THE SLIDE CHANGES.

_____**SLIDE**_____ LIZ, REACHING FOR THE

CAMERA, LAUGHING, HALF COVERED BY THE APPROACHING HAND.

MARTY   (RISING FROM HIS SEAT) Jesus.

JOSIE   Marty?

MUM   Language!

MARTY   (AS HE MOVES TOWARDS THE PROJECTION) Is that…

CLACK AS THE SLIDE CHANGES.

_____**SLIDE**_____ A FAMILY PORTRAIT. AWKWARD AND OLD.

MARTY   Go back.

CLACK AS THE SLIDE CHANGES.

_____**SLIDE**_____ MUM AND DAVID, KISSING CLOSE.

MARTY   The other way! Go back!

CLACK, CLACK AS THE SLIDE CHANGES BACK TWICE.

ALTHOUGH WE PASS THE PREVIOUS SLIDE, THE SLIDE WE STOP ON IS NOT THE SAME ONE AS BEFORE. IT IS, HOWEVER, THE SAME GIRL.

_____**SLIDE**_____ LIZ

KYLE   Martin?

MARTY   She looks… How did you get this?

MUM   Who is she?

KYLE   She was…

MARTY   How did you get this?

CLACK AS THE SLIDE CHANGES.

NOT THE SAME SLIDE AS BEFORE. THIS IS ONE WITH LIZ AS WELL.

_____**SLIDE**_____ LIZ.

KYLE   She was Martin's first girlfriend.

JOSIE   Really?

MARTY   She wasn't my... How did you get these? I mean, that's... I didn't know any of you...

JOSIE   Who was she?

MARTY   (LOST IN REVERIE) Liz. Her name was Liz.

CLACK AS THE SLIDE CHANGES.

_____**SLIDE**_____ THE FAMILY CAR. DAD BEHIND THE WHEEL, PROUD.

MUM   Who was she?

KYLE   She die...

MARTY   She didn't die.

KYLE   You told me she died?

MARTY   I was seventeen! I was heartbroken. She was my first love. The first... (SILENCE)

JOSIE   Martin?

AS MARTY SPEAKS THE SLIDES PERIODICALLY CHANGE, SHOWING THE COUPLE TOGETHER IN PERSONAL MOMENTS, ALWAYS, VERY UN-PHOTO-LIKE.

_____**SLIDE**_____ 3 TO 5 SLIDES. THE HISTORY OF LIZ AND MARTY.

MARTY   I was seventeen. I'd just moved into the bedsit. Do you remember? I told you it was because of work but actually... When we met, I was working at the car place. Remember? I was washing them. Driving BMWs back and forth for people I thought were... She... Her father had a 3 Series. Nice one. New at the time. He was a regular customer of ours and I... I'm not telling this very well. We met. We fell in

28

love. She was… she was beautiful. She had these eyes, so full, so round, and I'd lose myself in them, you know? I'd lose myself. Every day at the yard. Every night in the bedsit. I was doing my A Levels in the tech and… She had this smell. Like meat. I know, I know, but in a good way, like bread. Fresh bread. She was seventeen. Most girls wore a bottle of perfume every night, but she wore… She smelled… fresh. And her hair…

KYLE   You told me she died!

MARTY   What was I going to tell you? Her father moved to Saudi Arabia. I… I'd been an idiot. I mean, this was my first girlfriend and, I'd been an idiot, I don't even remember what. Not paying her enough attention, I suppose. I had this angel fall into my lap and I didn't know what I had… Her father moved to the Middle East. The whole family with him. She was mad at me. I thought she'd stay.

KYLE   Yeah, but… died.

MARTY   I was seventeen. I was seventeen and I'd just realized that things don't last. It felt like she did.

DAD CLICKS AT THE SLIDE BUT IT COMES UP BLANK.

QUIETLY JOSIE GOES BACK AND TALKS TO KYLE, WHO POINTS UP THE STAIRS. JOSIE GOES, BUT INTO THE KITCHEN RATHER THAN UP THE STAIRS.

DAD   That's the last one in the batch.

MUM   (EXITING TO THE KITCHEN) I'll put the kettle on.

JOSIE   I'll help.

JOSIE AND MUM GO INTO THE KITCHEN, CLEARING AWAY.

EXIT JOSIE / MUM.

BOB   Well, it's getting late… Sarah?

DAD   I'll get another batch.

DAVID   I think that's enough for now, yeah.

DAD   It'll only take a minute.

BOB   We've got wedding plans.

DAVID   Another night.

ENTER MUM.

MUM   You're not going?

DAVID   Another night.

DAD   Tomorrow then.

BOB   We've got the practice.

DAD   After the practice.

DAVID   Thanks for the... Martin. Good to see you
back here.

MARTY   Hmm?

DAVID   Good to see you back here.

MARTY   David.

ENTER JOSIE.

SARAH   Good night.

JOSIE   Good night. Congratulations.

JOSIE EXITS AND HEADS UPSTAIRS.

MARTY   (TO KYLE) Where's Josie?

SARAH   (PAUSING AT THE DOOR) I really
enjoyed... (SHE TRAILS OFF)

BOB   Sarah.

DAVID   I'll make sure they get back safely.

EXIT DAVID, SARAH, AND BOB.

DAD   Einstein invented the cat flap. Did you know
that? Florence Nightingale invented the pie chart.

MARTY   Is she upstairs?

DAD   Einstein…

KYLE   We heard you, Dad.

MUM   Let her go for a minute.

MARTY   (PAUSE) How did you get those photos anyway?

DAD   Einstein invented the cat flap. His voice started fission. Rutherford, Hahn. Bahr. Oppenheimer. Then they killed all the cats. I suppose they did, anyway; Schrödinger.

MARTY   I don't remember anyone taking pictures.

MUM   It was so long ago. What does it matter?

KYLE   I'll clean up.

MARTY   I just didn't know. That's all.

MUM   Oh, Martin. There are always things we don't know.

MARTY   (PAUSE; TO DAD) Kyle says you're reading Rainwater.

KYLE   Blue Rainbow.

MARTY   Kyle says you're reading it.

DAD   I haven't got time for fiction. Did you know, when they uncovered the Nazi experiments into fission? After the war. When they discovered the labs they were working in, they weren't even protected for the radiation. Can you imagine that?

MARTY   I'm not fiction.

DAD   That's how little they knew.

MUM   Martin…

MARTY   You're not reading it then?

DAD   What? What did you say? You mumble. I was never able to understand you when you mumble.

MARTY   You heard.

MUM   Don't start!

MARTY   I said; I'm not fiction.

DAD   Your books are though!

MARTY   But I'm not.

DAD   I'll read it.

MARTY   Don't bother.

DAD   No. I'll read it. Rainwater.

MUM   You know he doesn't read.

MARTY   Beethoven was deaf.

DAD   He lost it with the bombs.

MARTY   And you heard that well enough!

MUM   Let it go. I've read it.

MARTY   He reads. He reads everything.

MUM   He never reads fiction.

DAD   Is the kettle on?

DAD GOES INTO THE KITCHEN, MARTY TO THE BOTTOM OF THE STAIRS.

KYLE   (TO MUM) What's happening tomorrow?

MUM   What do you mean?

MARTY   (CALLING UP STAIRS) Josie?

KYLE   Uncle Bob said…

MUM   They're doing the practice tomorrow. For the wedding.

MARTY   Sweetheart, you okay?

KYLE   (STRANGELY   OVERWROUGHT)   I
thought we were doing Dad's thing?

MUM   It's a wedding, Kyle.

MARTY   What's this?

MUM   Kyle's getting all bent out of shape…

KYLE   I'm not. Listen, I don't care… They come in
here and hijack everything, you know what I mean? So she's
getting married, so what?

MARTY   Kyle…

KYLE   No, seriously, they come in here and hijack
everything. This was supposed to be a family thing, For Dad. For
his birthday! We've been organizing this for months!

MUM   It's a wedding!

KYLE   She hasn't said one word to us for, what, like,
ten years? Where've they been, eh? I don't even see how you can
invite them here! I can't! I mean, Jesus, it's not enough… I don't
see how you can invite them here! They just come in and take
over. Like that!

MUM   They're family!

MARTY   Mum.

KYLE   They're not family. I'm family. Marty's family.
Dad… They're not family. Not to me. I don't know how you
can invite them here. Really. I don't. It's… Fuck it.

HE TURNS TO GO.

MARTY   Kyle!

KYLE   No, fuck it. That's the way you want it, fine.

EXIT KYLE.

MARTY   He's got a point.

MUM   He's my brother, Marty. He's family, alright?

Family looks after one another. That's just the way it is.

MARTY   (GOING BACK TO THE STAIRS)
Sweetheart? (TO MUM) What were those photos doing in
there anyway?

MUM   You know your father.

MARTY'S CONFUSED BY THIS.

MARTY   (UP THE STAIRS) Josie?

MUM   There's something so... I don't know, about
weddings. It's family. Family together. The flowers, the church;
you know that church smell? There's nothing else like it, is there;
do you think they use special polish or something? You don't
get that in any other place. Not the men's clubs... not there. But
you get it in church, don't you? That smell. Holy smell I guess.
(PAUSE) And the dress. I think that's it for me. The dress. You get
it with the dress, don't you? White and everything. A new start.
A beginning. Clean slate and all that. I don't know.

MARTY   You haven't met him?

MUM   Who?

MARTY   The husband.

MUM   Not personally, no. Does it matter?

MARTY   I just think it's strange, that's all.

MUM   (ACCUSATIVELY) Well, we don't have much
to do with that side of the family. Not these days. Do we?

JOSIE COMES DOWN THE STAIRS.

MARTY   (TO JOSIE) You okay?

JOSIE   Yeah. Just needed... you know.

MUM   I'll see if your father needs a hand in the
kitchen.

EXIT MUM.

MARTY   I'm sorry about that. It's just…

JOSIE   No, please. Don't worry about it.

MARTY   It just took me by…

JOSIE   Don't worry about it.

MARTY   I didn't know they were going to be in there.

JOSIE   She was pretty.

MARTY   I guess. Yes. Suppose she's like a house now.

JOSIE   No. You can always tell, you know? In the cheekbones? It's all there. Whatever that person's going to look like in say, twenty to thirty years, it's all there in the cheekbones. Put on weight, don't put on weight. It doesn't matter. You can always tell. Good cheekbones and it doesn't matter what happens to them. They'll always look good.

MARTY   I suppose. I think we always used to look at the mother.

JOSIE   You never looked her up?

MARTY   Well, there was the whole 'death' thing.

JOSIE   Yeah, that was pretty dumb.

MARTY   No, I thought about it, you know, but there's that thing, when you're young. You know what I mean? You think, I don't know, life's a plot or something. Like it's all going to link up at the end. Tied in a neat little bow. Resolved. I thought, stupid really, but I thought we'd, I don't know, bump into one another or something. Sometime.

JOSIE   You know what I've always wanted, after you die?

MARTY   No, what?

JOSIE   I've wanted there to be a, I don't know. A movie or something. You get to sit down and each and every person who you've, you know, connected with in some way, you sit down and watch your life from their point of view. You know, just the bits that involve you. Lovers, friends, family. Everyone. You get to know exactly what was going on with them, what it was like to walk in their shoes. Why they, you know, did what they did, said what they said, you know what I mean?

MARTY   Sounds pretty horrible if you ask me.

JOSIE   Yeah? I don't know. See what it was like to walk in their shoes.

MARTY   Maybe they hated you.

JOSIE   Or maybe they really were looking out for your best interests, you know what I mean? I think it would be nice, you know. To see it all from their perspective. Know everything that was going on. Tie a little bow on it all.

MARTY   You're not staying then.

JOSIE   I've got my own family.

MARTY   Just, you know, for the weekend or something.

JOSIE   (KISSING HIM GOODBYE) I don't think so. (SHE GATHERS HER BAGS) You know, you should have found her. Really. That kind of thing... You got to be the narrator if you want it to be a story. (PAUSE) It was good to know you, understand?

MARTY   Need me to drive you?

JOSIE   I'll be fine. Give my best to your folks, yeah?

EXIT JOSIE.

BLACKOUT.

END OF ACT 1.

ACT 2

ACT 2

THE LIVING ROOM. AS BEFORE BUT NOW IT'S LATE NIGHT, THE HOUSE ASLEEP.

BEFORE LIGHTS UP WE SEE SLIDES APPEARING ON THE BACK WALL, ACCOMPANIED BY THE CLACK OF THE SLIDE PROJECTOR.

THE SLIDES – EIGHT TO TEN IN NUMBER – ARE OF RANDOM FAMILY EVENTS BUT INTERSPERSED WITH PICTURES OF SARAH, BOTH AS A YOUTH AND AT LEAST ONE OF HER WEDDING. ANOTHER, SHOWING AN OVEN, COMES UP BEFORE LIGHTS UP.

LIGHTS UP ON SARAH, SITTING ALONE ON THE COUCH.

PEERING INTENTLY FORWARD, AS THOUGH LOOKING AT THE SLIDES, SHE PAUSES AT THE OVEN AND GETTING UP, GOES TO THE EDGE OF THE STAGE, REACHING UP AS THOUGH TOUCHING THE OVEN, HER HAND BREAKING THE LIGHT OF THE SLIDE SO THAT IT APPEARS AS A SHADOW ON THE IMAGE BEHIND.

ENTER MARTY.

MARTY COMES DOWN THE STAIRS. WOKEN BY THE NOISE HE'S DRESSED IN PYJAMAS OR THE LIKE.

CLACK AS THE SLIDE CHANGES.

SLIDE RANDOM FAMILY SLIDE. NO SARAH.

SARAH, SO INTENT ON THE PICTURES, DOESN'T MOVE. MARTY, HOWEVER, RELAXES. HE GOES TO THE KITCHEN AND RETRIEVES TWO BEERS FROM THE FRIDGE BEFORE GOING ACROSS TO SARAH AND SITTING IN A CHAIR NEXT TO HER, OFFERING

A BEER WHICH SHE TAKES.

CLACK AS THE SLIDE CHANGES.

_____**SLIDE**_____ SARAH. EIGHT. ON A SWING.

SARAH   I remember this.

MARTY   Where is that?

SARAH   It's my friend, Elena's place. I'm… eight, I think.

MARTY   Why do we have so many pictures of you? I don't even think we saw you that year.

SARAH   We were living in the city. She had this house. Just in the suburbs. She was… She had this raven black hair. Raven. Night. She… We'd just moved there. End of the summer. She used to take this comb to school with her. White. We were girls. Hair was… well, it was important, and she had this white comb. Three times, every morning. Before classes. She'd brush her hair, top to bottom, top to bottom. Three times before class, three times after. She was… the most beautiful thing I think I'd seen. And she had this house, out in the suburbs, and she asked me over, you know, the new girl and everything? She asked me over and it was still daylight savings and there was this swing…

MARTY   Good memory. She took the picture?

SARAH   I was so happy there. At that time. The swing, we used to swing really high on it, but it was on mud, you understand? And, well, it moved. If you got high enough it moved. Tilted I guess it was. The other girls… there were always other girls… the other girls would only go so high, you understand? They'd swing and swing but if they got too high they'd stop kicking and maybe I wanted to show off, or maybe I didn't but I didn't care about that. The swing. I'd just keep on kicking. Even when the tension gave at the top, you remember? How the chain would go slack?

MARTY   The apex.

SARAH   I'd keep on kicking. (PAUSE) So happy. And

she'd watch me, you know? In the twilight. Just as the sun was coming down and she'd watch me. So happy.

MARTY   What happened.

SARAH   I fell off, of course. The chain broke I think. Or slipped its hook, I can't remember. We were good friends by then. She'd let me... at times she'd let me comb her hair. (BEAT) But it broke its chain and, I don't know. I hit my head I suppose. See? (SHE RAISES HER HAIR TO SHOW MARTY A SCAR; MARTY NODS) Hit it on the bar. Anyway, there was all this blood and I... I guess I thought I was dying or something because her mother called an ambulance rather than just driving me and there was this big fuss and she called my dad and...

PAUSE.

MARTY   Funny how these things stay with you.

SARAH   I couldn't go back. Not after that. But soon. I couldn't go back. And we had to move again.

SILENCE.

MARTY   Josie left.

SARAH   She was pretty.

MARTY   Thank you.

SARAH   Raven hair.

MARTY   She said she had her own family.

SARAH NODS.

MARTY   (CONT.) So, marriage, huh?

CLACK AS THE SLIDE CHANGES.

_____**SLIDE**_____ RANDOM AND INNOCUOUS FAMILY SLIDES.

SARAH   Yes.

MARTY   Marriage.

SARAH   Yes.

MARTY   I don't know. I mean, after... I don't know, maybe she reinforced it or something but I'm not sure I can ever see myself as getting married. Not really. I mean, if she, and of course by she I don't mean, she; I mean anyone, but I just can't see myself doing it if you know what I mean.

SARAH   I'm sure she loved you.

MARTY   What makes you say that?

SARAH SHRUGS.

MARTY   (CONT.) No, I mean, you know, marriage in general. I was lying up there, you know, in a bed that's about five times smaller than it was last time I slept in it, if you catch my drift, and I'm thinking; marriage. There's... You know, if there's one thing I've learnt through life is that there's no permanence. Nothing. Change is absolute, so you know, what's the point in trying to create something? And let's face it, that's what marriage is, isn't it? Trying to create something permanent out of something that was never meant to be. People; we're all just, you know, passing through, aren't we. When it all comes down to it. The illusion of permanence... I don't know. It's as though you signed yourself to someone in the hope that, you know, that'll all make it worth it or something. Tell me there's a marriage where they die in each others' arms and never thought about leaving each other? Tell me that, and I'll get married tomorrow.

SARAH   Perhaps it's not about that.

MARTY   Well, no, not for you obviously, I mean, I'm sure you'll be very happy and everything...

_____**SLIDE**_____ SLIDE OF THE CAR CRASH.

CLACK AS THE SLIDE CHANGES.

_____**SLIDE**_____ SLIDE OF DAVID, WAVING AT THE CAMERA, HOLDING MARTY'S HAND. MARTY IS AGED ABOUT ELEVEN.

MARTY STANDS AND MOVES TO THE EDGE OF THE STAGE.

MARTY   Oh, god. I remember this. This was… Where was this… I've got the strongest… You were there, weren't you? You… you were with Mum. She's taking this… you were…

SARAH   I was just a baby.

MARTY   That's right, you were. Bob left you with us for…

SARAH   For the summer.

MARTY   That's right, I remember. This… There's something about this, isn't there? Something missing.

SARAH   Kyle.

MARTY   That's…

SILENCE.

MARTY   (BITTERLY) David came with us. We went… I don't remember where we went. Just the four of us. Dad was… He was on one of his train trips wasn't he? He was… David had one of those cars, the ones where you could raise or lower the suspension. A Princess. An Austin Princess. I remember now. He had a Princess and we put you in the baby seat. It was… There was this big concert on the radio, you know, one of those charity things where millions of bands across the world are involved. Pretty normal now, but I guess that must have been one of the first ones because I wanted to listen to it, on the radio. I was so annoyed. David liked jazz and he'd put together, I don't know why, a Billy Holiday compilation, as if that's what ten year olds are into. Jesus. He just kept playing and singing at the top of his voice. I got… I think I got about ten minutes of concert. Mum kept shushing me and looking at him in the rear-view mirror…

SARAH   He was in love. You were young and he was in love. It wasn't his fault. He'd spent hours making the tape, simply hours. They were… They used to go dancing, when they were young, before she married your father. They used to go dancing. This was his way of telling her he still loved her. Across the headrest. And you kept talking about this band and that band and why it was important to the world… He was in love. This was how he showed it. How he proved it.

MARTY   (SOFTLY) Sarah… You know your… Uncle Bob…

ENTER KYLE.

KYLE COMES DOWN THE STAIRS FULL TILT, A HEAVY OBJECT IN HIS HANDS. HE SLAMS ON THE SWITCH, BATHING THE ROOM IN LIGHT ONCE MORE, FADING THE SLIDE. HE'S CLEARLY EXPECTING TO FIND BURGLARS.

KYLE   Jesus!

MARTY   (SHADING HIS EYES) Aw, fuck. Kyle! What the fuck!

KYLE   Jesus. You scared the shit out of me!

MARTY   We're just having a beer!

KYLE   What's she doing here?

MARTY   Getting the shit scared out of her, it seems. Turn that light off!

KYLE OBLIGES.

KYLE   I thought someone had broken in.

MARTY   And decided to go through the family slides?

KYLE   I was asleep.

MARTY   Yeah, well. Go back up there, if you like.

KYLE   'M awake now. Where'd you get the beer.

MARTY   Fridge.

CLACK AS THE SLIDE CHANGES.

KYLE GOES TO THE FRIDGE.

_____**SLIDE**_____ BARNEY, THE DOG.

KYLE   Barney again.

MARTY   (GOING TO THE PROJECTOR) I want to know where those slides came from before.

KYLE   The ones of the dead girl.

MARTY   I want to know where they came from.

KYLE   (JOKING) Beyond the grave.

MARTY   Will you shut up about that! I want to know where they came from.

SARAH   The box was empty. When I came in. I had to reload.

MARTY   You changed cartridges?

SARAH   It was empty when I came in.

MARTY   If I'm going to lose a girlfriend over this then I'd like to know who took them.

KYLE   You didn't lose anything.

MARTY   Says mister single.

KYLE   I mean she didn't leave you because of the photos. She had to go home. Nothing more.

MARTY   Yeah, well, I'd like to know.

SARAH   Kyle?

KYLE   What.

SARAH   Would you like to see something?

KYLE   Like what?

SARAH   I found it before. Just before Marty came down. I'm sure I can find it again. Would you like to see it?

KYLE   What is it?

SARAH GETS UP AND GOES TO THE PROJECTOR.

SARAH   I'm sure I can find it.

KYLE   (ASIDE, TO MARTY) Fuck is she doing here?

MARTY   Leave her alone.

KYLE   I thought she was in practice or something.

MARTY   I don't know. I just found her sitting here. Does she have a key?

KYLE   She weirds me out.

MARTY   She's, she's just a little messed up is all. You know, before the wedding and everything. Listen, she's got this crackpot idea about Mum...

SARAH   I've found it!

CLACK AS THE SLIDE CHANGES.

_____**SLIDE**_____ A CHURCH TOWER SEEN THROUGH A CARAVAN WINDOW.

THE BOYS MOVE DOWNSTAGE, LOOKING AT THE PHOTO. BOTH SEEM TO RECOGNIZE IT FROM SOMEWHERE. KYLE IS THE MORE ENTRANCED.

KYLE   What is that?

MARTY   Was that..? Do you remember that camp Mum used to send us to, the religious one?

KYLE   Wrong style.

MARTY   There was that church in the centre of the village.

KYLE   It's the wrong style, I'm telling you. That's Gothic, this is more, I don't know, Nicholas Hawksmoor.

SARAH   Is he a member of the family?

MARTY   He's... no. He was... Dad had this thing about churches. Architecture. He used to drag us miles... Do you remember that time in Leeds? Kyle?

KYLE   Yeah, yeah.

MARTY   We walked through Leeds at about one a.m. just to go look at this old church. There was… This police car came tearing round the corner and bumped up on the kerb next to us, both doors fly open and they start chasing this guy down the street. Just left us standing next to the car; doors open, siren wailing. That was Hawksmoor I think.

SARAH   Who was he?

MARTY   He was… He's an architect. Was. Designed churches. After the…

KYLE   (REFERRING TO THE PHOTO) I know this.

MARTY   … after the Great Fire of London, I think it was, he was commissioned to build five churches across London. Which, it is said, form a pentacle across the city.

SARAH   Really?

MARTY   I thought you'd like that.

KYLE   I know this.

ENTER MUM.

MUM   Can't you guys keep it down, your father is trying to sleep.

MARTY   Mum, do you recognize this?

MUM   I haven't got my glasses.

KYLE   I swear I know this.

MARTY   We were just going through some of the slides.

MUM   (COMING CLOSER) Your father's trying to sleep. Hello Sarah.

MARTY   Kyle seems to think it's Hawksmoor.

MUM   That's the caravan isn't it? I remember that latch. Even when we were kids it wouldn't shut. I used to have a bed on that side, when we stayed at the farm, and the window wouldn't latch properly. We had to, you know, stuff it with something to stop the rain coming in.

DURING THIS KYLE HAS TURNED AWAY. HE IS STARING STRAIGHT AT SARAH IN CONTEMPT. SARAH HOLDS HIS EYE WITH AN OPEN FACE.

ONLY MUM DOESN'T SEEM TO KNOW THE SIGNIFICANCE OF THIS.

KYLE   You're sick, you know that.

SARAH   It was in the pile.

THE DOORBELL RINGS INSISTENTLY.

MUM   (TO THE DOOR) Shush!

DAD   (OFF) What's going on down there!

MUM   (TO THE STAIRS) It's just the boys!

MARTY GOES TO OPEN THE DOOR.

MARTY   (TO MUM) Jesus, Mum.

SARAH   (STANDING) I guess I should go.

DAD   (OFF) Who's down there!

MARTY   (TO THE DOOR AS HE OPENS IT) Shut the hell up!

THE DOOR OPENS AND BOB WALKS IN.

BOB   Where is she?

MUM   Robert?

MARTY   She has a key but he doesn't?

BOB   (SEEING THE SLIDE ON THE WALL; TO SARAH) Go wait outside for me!

MARTY	Take it easy, Bob.
MUM	Robert, what's the matter?
BOB	Go wait outside! Now!

ENTER DAD.

SARAH TURNS TO EXIT AND STOPS, LOOKING BACK INTO THE ROOM.

SARAH	I had a lovely time. Really.

EXIT SARAH.

DAD	What's going on!
MARTY	Listen, Bob…
BOB	Uncle Bob. Uncle Bob. You understand?!
MARTY	It's three o'clock in the morning!
KYLE	(SUDDENLY) She's twenty-three! She's twenty-three.
DAD	What the hell's going on, Bob?
MUM	Robert..!
BOB	Don't think I don't know what's going on!
DAD	I was asleep!

BOB   Don't think I don't know what's going on! I know what you're up to! All of you.

MUM	Robert…
BOB	All of you! She comes over here…
MARTY	Why don't we all try to…

BOB   She has a key, does she? She has a key! Don't think I don't know what's going on! I'm on to you, see. I know what your tricks are. I know what you're thinking. And I'm not having it, do you understand me? I'm not having it! Keep away from her, you understand me? Keep away! And, you know what, you're not invited. All of you! Don't come tomorrow morning. Don't come to the wedding. You understand me. None of you! You're not invited!

MUM	Robert.
BOB	None of you.
MARTY	Bob, listen, I don't know what you think…

BOB   None of you! You're not invited. None of you! Weddings are for family and family look out for one another.

KYLE	She's twenty-three!
BOB	Stay away from her.
MARTY	I think you'd better leave.
BOB	Stay away from her. I'm telling you!

EXIT BOB.

DAD	(AFTER A PAUSE) I'm going to bed.
MARTY	Kyle.
MUM	Father!
DAD	I'm going to bed.

EXIT DAD.

MUM WAITS A SECOND AND THEN FOLLOWS HIM UP THE STAIRS.

MARTY	Kyle!
KYLE	Leave it.
MARTY	Listen…
KYLE	Just… Just leave it, alright? Let it the fuck alone.
MARTY	Listen…

KYLE   Oh, fuck off, why don't you? Just… Why'd you even have to come here anyway?

MARTY	(PAUSE) I'm going to bed.
KYLE	Fine.
MARTY	I'll see you in the morning, alright?
KYLE	Just fuck off and go.
MARTY	Turn the projector off when you're done.

EXIT MARTY.

KYLE SITS DOWN ON THE COUCH, A MIRROR OF THE START OF THE ACT.

HE REACHES UP AND TURNS THE PROJECTOR OFF, PLUNGING THE ROOM INTO DARKNESS.

CURTAINS.

END OF ACT 2.

ACT 3

ACT 3

CURTAINS ON THE LIVING ROOM, EARLY MORNING.

DAVID IS STANDING BY THE DINING TABLE. HE'S GOT A BOX OF SLIDES AND IS TAKING THEM OUT, ONE BY ONE, AND HOLDING THEM UP TO THE LIGHT.

ENTER GRANDMA.

GRANDMA ENTERS CARRYING A CUP OF TEA AND SOME TOAST FOR DAVID.

GRANDMA   Here you go, sweetheart, get this down you.

DAVID   Thank you. This looks… It's all lovely, thank you.

GRANDMA   You find what you were looking for?

DAVID   Some of it. Yes. You know there's one of you in here.

GRANDMA   Is that right?

DAVID HOLDS UP A SLIDE FOR HER TO SEE.

GRANDMA   Would you look at that!

DAVID   It was that time… I think I was, what fifteen? I came round and you made…

GRANDMA   Tea.

DAVID   You remember?

GRANDMA   Of course I remember. I always liked you David. We both did. You were a sweet young man. Do you remember that tree in the garden?

DAVID   The one with the swing?

GRANDMA   That's the one. I used to see you out there, sitting in it. Never in autumn, mind you. In summer. I used to watch you watching the house, you were very sweet.

DAVID   I was very young.

GRANDMA   We all were. Once. You remember the balloon?

DAVID   There was one of that in here. Somewhere. I just saw it.

HE RIFLES THROUGH THE PACK AND PULLS OUT A SLIDE.

DAVID   (CONT.) Here.

GRANDMA   Well. There it is. Fantastic.

DAVID   It took me about… I think I spent a week just looking for that.

GRANDMA   It was very sweet of you.

DAVID   She didn't like it, though.

GRANDMA   No, she liked it well enough. She liked it alright. It just scared her a bit, you understand? You were so intense back then. Always was. It came, like you planned, on the morning of her graduation and it, well, it worked just like you thought it would. She opened the box – she must have known it was from you, you know, the British postmark and everything – anyway, she opened it and up the balloon went, just like you intended it.

DAVID   I wasn't sure about the air pressure. I thought, with the plane and everything. Helium disperses at the certain height, or becomes thinner or something like that, and I wasn't sure it would work, you know after all that way. I thought it might just be a limp piece of foil at the bottom of the box.

GRANDMA   It wasn't. It went right up. Out of the box and up to the ceiling. Just like you planned. 'Good Luck.' It was very sweet of you.

DAVID   She never said anything about it. Not then. Not til later.

GRANDMA   You scared her. In America, you understand.

Four thousand miles and you reached out and touched her. It was like the tree thing. You were just there. Whether she wanted you to be or not. Sweet is sweet but girls don't usually want sweet. Girls of that age want sour. They've had the sweet since they were old enough to walk. Teenagers want a bit of tang, if you follow my meaning.

DAVID   I suppose.

SHE PATS HIS HAND AND RISES, MOVING BACK TO THE KITCHEN.

ENTER MARTY.

GRANDMA   Tea?

MARTY   Um. Hi. Sorry?

GRANDMA   Would you like some tea?

MARTY   Coffee, if you've got it.

EXIT GRANDMA.

MARTY SITS AT THE TABLE.

MARTY   (CONT.) David.

DAVID   Long night?

MARTY   You wouldn't believe. Why aren't you at the practice?

DAVID   I wasn't invited.

MARTY   Yeah, well. Us too, it seems.

DAVID   Pictures are wonderful things don't you think? Pictures? Slides especially. You never know what's on them, do you? Slides? They're just these little white boxes with black in the middle but; 'click' and there you have it. A complete picture.

MARTY   I'll be honest. I didn't even know they made them anymore. I mean. What's the point, right? JPEGS... I thought everyone just ran them off the computer you know?

DAVID   I have a lot of photos. You know? I never had a family. You know that. I never had children, like your mother. And I liked it, most of the time. Living alone. It's refreshing, I think. Being alone. And I never had people round, not really, but I had lots of photos.

MARTY   I remember.

DAVID   The walls.

MARTY   Black and white. Always black and white. What was with that?

DAVID   Things are better in black and white.

MARTY   (QUOTING) Kodachrome.

DAVID   You see. That's the problem. These days. With computers. The whole picture's so perfect, so detailed, it's not a memory, it's… I don't know, movies or something. Freeze frame. Memory's not like that. Memory's imperfect. Faulty. You can't see everything clearly. Not all the time, and half the time you don't even know what you're seeing. You can see each bit of the picture individually but never the whole thing. Black and white's like that. It draws the eye. (HOLDING UP A SLIDE) Look. See? I'll show you.

HE GOES OVER TO THE PROJECTOR AND TURNING IT ON PUTS THE SLIDE IN.

I'll show you, you'll see. Give it some time.

MARTY   It's a song you know. Kodachrome. It's a song by Paul Simon. What I meant before? "Everything looks worse in black and white?"

DAVID IGNORES HIM.

ENTER GRANDMA.

SHE PUTS THE COFFEE ON THE TABLE FOR MARTY.

GRANDMA   What's he doing?

MARTY   Thanks. I honestly wasn't paying attention.

_____ **SLIDE** _____ A SEAFRONT.

DAVID   See! There. See the shadows? That line there?
What is that.

MARTY   (NOT CARING) I don't know. A boat or
something I suppose.

DAVID   It could be. It could be. It might very well be a
boat. There might be people on that boat. That might have been
a fisherman. A couple on vacation or something.

MARTY   Where is that?

DAVID   Pembroke.

MARTY   Not likely to be a vacation then.

DAVID   Perhaps. Perhaps not. Maybe it's not even a
boat. Maybe it's sunlight. You know, transposing. What time of
day do you think that is?

MARTY   I'm not sure.

DAVID   You can't tell. You can't see it. Why was it even
taken?

MARTY   I get what you're saying.

DAVID   Maybe it's a scratch on the film. The Loch Ness
Monster.

MARTY   On vacation.

DAVID   The point is it's imperfect. Incomplete.
Beautiful. (PAUSE) I studied photography? You know that?

MARTY   I didn't. No.

DAVID   In university. Hence the pictures.

MARTY   I thought you just liked taking photos.

EXIT GRANDMA.

DAVID   Three years. You know what I learnt? There were two types of people. Photographers. One; they like the technique. The aperture, the soft focus. They read all the manuals they can get their hands on and they get all the technology they can. Wide lenses, zoom lenses, it doesn't matter. Every piece they can. The others; they don't care about any of that. They focus on the film. Bend it, stretch it, freeze it, subject it to as many different light sources as they can. I think life's like that.

MARTY   I thought it was all composition.

DAVID   That's art. The end product. I'm talking about how you take the picture.

MARTY   David. The photos... Last night... Liz... Did you put those in there?

ENTER KYLE.

KYLE   What time is it?

MARTY   Nine.

KYLE   In the morning?

MARTY   Jesus, man. You stink! What did you drink?

KYLE   Mum's bottle.

DAVID   Crème de cacao?

KYLE   Hey David.

MARTY   Yeah, well. That'll teach you.

KYLE   Why am I up?

MARTY   There's coffee in the kitchen.

KYLE GETS UP AND GOES TOWARDS THE KITCHEN. HE'S JUST ABOUT TO ENTER WHEN HE STOPS, NOTICING SMOKE COMING OUT OF THE KITCHEN.

KYLE   Shit!

DAVID AND MARTY TURN AND LOOK TOWARDS

THE KITCHEN. SEEING THE GATHERING SMOKE THEY JUMP OUT OF THEIR SEATS.

ENTER MUM AND DAD.

MUM AND DAD COME DOWN THE STAIRS WITH AN AIR OF POST COITAL GLOW ABOUT THEM. DAVID, FORGETTING THE FIRE, NOTICES THIS.

A FIRE ALARM GOES OFF.

MARTY   Where's the extinguisher?

KYLE   Next to the cooker.

MARTY   Great!

DAD   What's going on down here?

MARTY   Where's the spare extinguisher.

MUM   In the garage.

MARTY   Kyle?

KYLE RUNS OUT THE GARAGE. MUM, PICKING UP A CLOTH OR SOMETHING SIMILAR, TRIES TO BLOW THE SMOKE AWAY FROM THE FIRE ALARM.

EXIT KYLE.

DAVID   Should I call the fire brigade!

MARTY   It's just the oven.

ENTER KYLE.

KYLE GIVES THE EXTINGUISHER TO MARTY.

KYLE   Here!

DAD   Give that here!

MARTY HALF ENTERS THE KITCHEN AND BLASTS THE FIRE EXTINGUISHER INTO THE ROOM. THE SMOKE DISSIPATES, THE FIRE GOES OUT.

DAVID   Good job, lad.

THE PHONE RINGS AND DAD PICKS IT UP.

MUM   Look at the kitchen! It's ruined!

DAD   (INTO THE PHONE))Hello?

DAVID   Let me see.

DAD   (INTO THE PHONE) Oh, Bob. What do you
want?

DAVID   It's nothing but soot. We'll have it cleaned up in
no time. Won't we boys?

DAD   (INTO THE PHONE) No, we've got a bit of
drama here.

KYLE   Speak for yourself.

MUM   Oh, look at the state… How can you boys be
so stupid!

DAD   (INTO THE PHONE, ANGER RISING)
Yeah, well, I'm sorry to hear that, Bob!

MARTY   Don't look at us! That girl you've got staying
here…

DAD   (INTO THE PHONE) I really don't think
you're in any position…

MUM   What in god's name are you talking about!

MARTY   The exchange student or whatever she is!

DAD   (INTO THE PHONE, SHOUTING) You
listen to me, Bob! No. You listen to me. I've put up with this
stuff for far too long…

MUM   (ANXIOUS) Is that, Bob?

DAD   (INTO THE PHONE) I'm not putting up
with it anymore! You hear me!?

MUM   Let me talk to him!

DAD   (INTO THE PHONE, TURNING HIS

BACK ON HER) We don't want to come to any stupid wedding. You understand? We wouldn't come if you begged us. After what you've done…

KYLE   Fucking bastard!

EXIT KYLE.

MUM   (MOVING TO FOLLOW HIM) Kyle!

DAD   (INTO THE PHONE) You don't call here. You don't talk to us. You got that? You and your crazy daughter! You understand me!

HE SLAMS THE PHONE DOWN.

MUM   Father!

MARTY   I'll check on Kyle then, shall I?

NO ONE PAYS ATTENTION AND HE HEADS OUT.

EXIT MARTY.

MUM   (MOVING TO THE PHONE) I'll talk to him.

DAD   (STOPPING HER) No, you won't!

MUM   He's my brother.

DAD   After the way he's treated this family!

MUM   He's my brother!

DAD   We're not even invited to the wedding. Not even an invite! Yesterday he's eating hamburgers off my barbecue, today we're not even invited to the wedding. As far as I'm concerned that's it! He's dead to us.

MUM   You know what he's like.

DAD   (BEAT) Fine. He's your brother. You deal with him!

EXIT DAD.

MUM STARES AT THE PHONE FOR A FEW SECONDS

UNDER THE WATCHFUL EYE OF DAVID, THEN
TURNS TO THE KITCHEN.

MUM   Such a mess!

DAVID   Here, we'll get it cleaned up, in no time.

HE GENTLY PUTS HIS HAND ON HER ARM BUT SHE
SHAKES HIM OFF.

MUM   No, David.

DAVID   Kim.

MUM   (FIRMLY) I said, no!

DAVID   Come here. I've got something to show you.

MUM   The kitchen…

DAVID   The fire's out.

MUM   Such a mess.

DAVID   (LEADING HER TO THE COUCH) Sit
here.

MUM   Oh, not more of these things.

DAVID   Just sit.

MUM   I never liked photos.

DAVID   You'll like these. Just sit for a second. Alright?

MUM   Your place always gave me the creeps. All those
faces watching. Judging.

DAVID   Watch this.

_____**SLIDE**_____ A BEACH.

MUM   What are we looking at?

DAVID   You don't remember?

MUM   (SUDDENLY INTERESTED) That's the
beach isn't it?

DAVID	Where we took the boys.
MUM	I don't have time for…

_____ **SLIDE** _____ A BEACH AGAIN. CLOSER.

MUM	I haven't thought about that in years.
DAVID	I have it on my wall.
MUM	Always you and that camera.
DAVID	Do you remember the donkey?
MUM	With the…
DAVID	Martin was…
MUM	Do you know, the male donkey has the largest… thing… amongst mammals.
DAVID	I thought that was sperm whales.
MUM	Proportionately.
DAVID	She was such a pretty young girl.
MUM	Who?

_____ **SLIDE** _____ SARAH AS A CHILD.

DAVID	Sarah.
MUM	God. I'd forgotten she was with us.
DAVID	Such a sweet young thing.
MUM	You were always sweet. I remember that. So… respectful.

_____ **SLIDE** _____ SARAH ON A DONKEY RIDE.

MUM	I'm sorry… I hurt you, didn't I.
DAVID	It doesn't matter.
MUM	He was…
DAVID	It's okay.

_____ **SLIDE** _____ MUM COMING OUT OF THE WATER, AFTER SWIMMING.

MUM   (LAUGHING) Oh, god. Look at me. I look a sight.

DAVID   You were beautiful.

MUM   Where did you get these?

DAVID   They were in the box.

MUM   Just in the box?

DAVID   Can you believe it?

MUM   I don't even remember you having the camera.

DAVID   Do you remember this?

_____ **SLIDE** _____ MUM WRAPPED IN A BLANKET, HELD TIGHT BY DAVID.

MUM   I did love you, you know. I want you to know that. I did.

DAVID   I know.

MUM   It wasn't just…

DAVID   It's okay.

MUM   He was such an… asshole. Two years? You know that? That's how long before I found out.

DAVID   I know all this.

MUM   It's just, the time, you know? The time. That's what I can't get my head around. Is it different for men? I don't think it is. I don't think it is different, I think it's just mean. I think it's just…

DAVID   He came back to you.

MUM   That summer. You know, I think it was the happiest in my life, do you know that? With you. Little Marty. Sarah. That was… I think that was as close to happiness as you can ever come.

DAVID   For me too.

_____**SLIDE**_____ A HOTEL, OLD.

MUM   Such a horrible place. You know what I mean? I mean, not horrible… and that hotel manager. The staff! God. When they were making Marty eat that porridge… and the rain. Jesus, I think it was probably the worst… You were always so good with the kids. I think. You should have become a father, you really should. You were always so good with the kids. I'm not sure we were. Not really. I think perhaps we were…

DAVID   It's easier when they're not yours. Easier. Different.

MUM   You would have made a wonderful father.

DAVID   Kim…

_____**SLIDE**_____ SARAH AGAIN, BEING PUT INTO A CAR BY MUM.

DAVID   (CONT.) There's something I need you to think about. I need to say it, and I think it's something you need to remember.

MUM   I don't want to talk about this…

DAVID   I know, but…

MUM   I don't want to talk about this!

DAVID   … it's important. (PAUSE) I need you to ask yourself, Kim, I need you to ask yourself why we took Sarah? Why did we take Sarah, Kim? Why did we leave Kyle with Bob and take Sarah.

MUM   The kitchen…

_____**SLIDE**_____ KYLE AS A BOY.

DAVID   It'll wait. I think you need to remember this.

MUM   He was… He always was. He was such a

sensitive boy.

DAVID   We left a seven year old with your brother and took a three year old with us? Don't you think there was something strange about that?

MUM   Martin could… As soon as he left, after, you know, after I found out about it. After the fight. Before I called you. He… He wouldn't stop crying. You know what I mean? Where's Daddy gone? When's Daddy coming back? Marty was always so… he could cope, you know what I mean? He could cope. Kyle… It seemed like the perfect idea, you know what I mean? Sarah was too young for camping. Even in a caravan. And Kyle needed a male figure… (PAUSE) I always wanted a girl. You know that? When I became… after we… I hoped that was a girl. (SHE SHRUGS) But, you know, those things happen. It's not easy being a woman in a house full of men. Not easy.

_____**SLIDE**_____ KYLE IN A BAR, YOUNGER, DRUNK, ANGRY.

MUM   And when he came back… when we came back and he was here, all… It seemed so straightforward, you know what I mean?

DAVID   Going back.

MUM   It all seemed so straightforward.

DAVID   Okay.

MUM   I shouldn't have left him.

DAVID   No.

MUM   It was just so…

_____**SLIDE**_____ A SERIES OF SLIDES SHOWING AN ALTERNATE PAST WHERE MUM AND DAVID WERE TOGETHER. ALL THE KIDS ARE THERE, AND MORE.

THE PAIR WATCH TOGETHER, ENTRANCED.

THEN THE SLIDES END. A SERIES OF CLICKS SHOW NOTHING BUT WHITE ON THE WALLS.

MUM RISES AND KISSES DAVID GENTLY BUT NOT DEEPLY.

THE PHONE RINGS AND MUM MOVES AWAY, PICKING IT UP.

MUM   (INTO PHONE) Hello?

DAVID SHUTS OFF THE POWER TO THE PROJECTOR.

MUM   (TO DAVID) It's Emily. (INTO PHONE) Where are you honey? (PAUSE) No, no. I understand. (PAUSE) Well, we're all here. David's here. We're… (PAUSE) Of course, I understand. No, I understand. (PAUSE) Well, we'll see you when you get here. (PAUSE) Alright. We love you too.

SHE HANGS UP.

ENTER MARTY AND KYLE.

MARTY ENTERS, CLEARLY ANGRY. KYLE FOLLOWS IN ANNOYED SUPPLICATION.

DAVID   Is she coming?

MUM   I think so, yes.

KYLE   Marty..!

MARTY   You're out of your fucking mind.

MUM   Marty!

KYLE   This is my life!

MARTY   (TO MUM) He wants to… (TO KYLE) Tell her what you want to do!

KYLE   It's my life! After what he did…

ENTER DAD.

DAD   (TO MARTY) Are you part of this family or not?

MARTY   Am I..? Am I part..!? What the hell is wrong with you people! I'm out of here!

KYLE   He deserves it. You saw him!

MARTY   It's wrong!

KYLE   He's wrong! He's wrong!!! He's... that sick fuck...

MUM   Kyle!

KYLE   I'm sorry, but are you my brother or are you not my brother!

MARTY   You're out of your goddamned mind!

DAD   Are you part of this family or are you not!

MUM   Daniel!

MARTY   (TO KYLE) Listen. I'm sorry. You're... He was wrong. Jesus, of course he was wrong! What do you expect me to say! He was wrong and we all know it! But what you want to do... It's a wedding. A wedding!

DAD   Which he never invited us to!

MARTY   Grow up.

MUM   Marty!

DAD   Don't you dare talk to me in that tone of voice. I brought you up, if it hadn't been for me...

MARTY   If it hadn't been for you? Where were you twenty years ago? Huh? Where were you when I came to you!?

DAD   I did what I thought was right!

MARTY   Right? Jesus! And this is right, is it?

DAD   He deserves...

MARTY   Bullshit! You don't give a shit about what he deserves or doesn't deserve. You... You're so full of shit, you know that!

MUM   Martin! I will not have that language in my house.

MARTY   (TO MUM) Ask him! Ask him what he wants to do?

MUM   Father?

MARTY   He wants to announce it. He wants to go to the wedding, no, he hasn't got the guts to do that himself, he wants Kyle to go to the wedding and when they say "does any man know reason" he wants him to stand up and tell everyone.

MUM   Oh, Daniel! No!

KYLE   It's my life!

DAD   Listen...

MARTY   (TO KYLE) Listen. I'm sorry. I... This guy deserves to be strung up by his balls for what he did. He deserves... but this is twenty years ago!

MUM   Oh, Kyle!

KYLE   And what about her!?

MARTY   Think about... Think about all the other people this happened to. George, Alan maybe... Think about Sarah!

KYLE   This is for her, this is for her! Look how she turned out!

MARTY   What if there's more? Eh. What if it's not just you and George? What if it's not just Sarah! What about our cousins, eh? What about Paul? He stayed there as well! What if what happened to you, happened to a lot of other people?

KYLE   This is for them!

MARTY   No it's not! I'm sorry, it's not! Paul... Paul's got a family! He's got kids, for Christ's sake. You think he wants all this dragged up again? Where do we take it, eh? Do we take it to court? Is that where we take it? To the press? Do we put it all out there in the open?

MUM   Marty!

MARTY   How many lives do you want to ruin with this?
What about Sarah!

DAD   This is a family, alright! And we stay together,
that sack of shit...

MARTY   Don't you dare. Don't you goddamn dare! I
told you! I told you! Twenty years ago! I came to you and told
you! What did you do?

DAD   I did what's best for the family!

MARTY   You banned him from the house! From the
house! Jesus! He was just a kid! Look at him! Look at Sarah!
And you want to stand up in her wedding and do that to her?
Do you? You ought to be ashamed of yourself.

MUM   Martin!

MARTY   And don't you start! You were so...

MUM   He's my brother!

MARTY   And he's mine! You understand that? You were
so busy getting... Listen, David, I'm sorry. You're a good guy and
everything but you're not family, no matter how much you want
to be, you're not. And (TO MUM) you were so busy.

MUM   Stop it!

MARTY   (TO KYLE) You know how many times
I thought about killing him? Do you? I went to bed every
night... There are no kids now. No grandchildren. No... He's
an old man. A sad old man, and this is her way out, do you get
that? She's getting married. Married. He's got nothing. Nothing.
I want him punished as much as you but this is just spite. And
I'm having nothing to do with it!

DAD   You are my son and...

MARTY   Which means?

DAD   What?

MARTY   What does that mean? Huh? David was more of a father to me growing up than… I'm not doing this. You're… You had a chance. One chance, twenty years ago to do something about this, to protect your family and you blew it, blew it!

DAD   When you have a family…!

MARTY   Oh, spare me the 'when you have a family' bullshit.

MUM   Marty!

DAD   When you have a family!!! You'll understand! You'll understand!

KYLE GOES AND SITS ON THE SOFA. UNBIDDEN THE SLIDES CLICK THROUGH.

_____**SLIDE**_____   THE CARAVAN.

_____**SLIDE**_____   KYLE AS A CHILD IN THE CORNER OF THE BED IN THE CARAVAN, HIS KNEES PULLED UP AGAINST HIM, CLEARLY CRYING.

_____**SLIDE**_____   BOB IS HELPING KYLE AS A CHILD OUT OF HIS SWEATER.

DAD   The responsibility..! He was kid. Just a little kid. He didn't know what was happening to him. He didn't know. He couldn't. This is your mother's brother we're talking about. Your uncle!? You wanted him to spend the rest of his life in jail? You wanted him to go through that. In there! You know what would have happened to him. He's your mother's brother. Half brother. He's family and family have got to stick together. How'd you know it didn't happen to you, eh? You were just a little kid! What makes you think it didn't happen to you!? What would you have had me do? Tell me that? What would you have had me do? Drag our family through that! The press… What would you have had me do?

MUM   (TO MARTY) Go wait in the garden. (TO DAVID) David?

DAVID   Come on, Marty.

DAD   What would you have had me do? Take her in? Take in another… You know how tight things were back then? Do you? You know the sacrifices your mother…

EXIT DAVID AND MARTY.

DAD   (TO MUM) What would he have had me do?

MUM   Talk to him.

DAD   He doesn't understand. He's too young.

MUM   Emily's coming.

DAD   Emily?

MUM   She called.

DAD   Today?

MUM   Talk to him. You do remember it's your birthday, don't you? Talk to him.

EXIT MUM.

DAD PAUSES AND THEN GOES AND SITS DOWN ON THE SOFA.

DAD   It's not called an aisle, you know. I don't know where they get that from, but it's not called an aisle. In a church. The aisle is the bit that runs round the side, you know, so people can get to their seats. They don't walk her down the aisle. Not in a church. It's called the central passageway.

KYLE   That right?

DAD   Emily's coming.

KYLE   I heard.

DAD   We named her after your grandmother, you know?

KYLE   I know.

DAD   Named you after my uncle. Scottish, I think. Only met him the once. That one time. Looked a bit like you mind. Purposeful. (PAUSE) Your mother thinks it'll be a bad idea with the wedding and everything. (KYLE NODS) But... you know...

KYLE   She's probably right.

DAD   Strange girl, really.

KYLE   Emily?

DAD   Emily? No. Emily... well, she was always your mother's favourite. No, Sarah.

KYLE   Yeah.

DAD   So... quiet. Even as a toddler.

KYLE   Wouldn't you be living with a sick fu...

DAD   We don't know that!

KYLE   I do. I can see it in her. Every time.

DAD   Kyle...

KYLE   I can. I can just see it in her.

DAD   My father. He had a bit of temper like. Used to hit me...

KYLE   It's not the same thing.

DAD   No.

KYLE   I think the projector's broken.

DAD   She was beautiful, I ever tell you that? I suppose not. Beauty is... You don't know what to do with it, you know what I mean? Beauty? It's just there, if you know what I mean. You don't know what to do with it apart from possess it. (BEAT) Guess that's why those people pay stupid money for paintings and stuff. Only thing to do with beauty is own it.

KYLE   You came back though.

DAD   I came back. Possession's one thing. Keeping's another.

KYLE   We should have done more for her. Sarah.

DAD   Things were tight. Bob'd... Your mother... after we got back together... there were debts, you understand? Can't live that way and not work. Bob'd lent us... Well, your mother asked him, I didn't know anything about it, of course, but your mother'd asked him to, you know, help us out and everything. Keep a roof over your heads. So...

KYLE   What time's she getting here?

DAD   Emily? Your mother didn't say.

KYLE   We doing it at lunch or dinner?

DAD   Dinner. I think.

KYLE   (HE SIGHS) Alright. (HE STANDS TO LEAVE) The projector's broken, I think.

EXIT KYLE.

DAD SITS ALONE ON THE SOFA FOR A SECOND BEFORE BLACKOUT, NOT SAD BUT REMEMBERING.

_____**SLIDE**_____ THE CARAVAN.

CURTAINS.

END OF ACT 3.

The Family

ACT 4

ACT 4

LIGHTS UP ON THE LIVING ROOM.

A DINNER TABLE IS CENTRE STAGE, THE PLACES SET FOR A BIG MEAL. A HAPPY BIRTHDAY SIGN IS ON THE WALL.

DAD IS FIDDLING WITH THE PROJECTOR, TRYING TO GET IT TO WORK. MUM IS BUSYING HERSELF ARRANGING THE TABLE. GRANDMA IS HELPING.

GRANDMA   You want salad forks?

MUM   On the left.

GRANDMA   I miss salad.

MUM   There's some in the kitchen.

GRANDMA   No. Real salad. Like back home.

MUM   We have real salad.

GRANDMA   With cheese in it. Real cheese. This country... It's so cold, you know what I mean? And no salad. I don't know how they can stand it.

MUM   Wasn't really 'salad' though, was it? Could you put that over there?

GRANDMA   Bacon bits. Cheese. They miss the whole idea of a salad over here.

MUM   Salad cream.

GRANDMA   Please! That's not real mayonnaise. Not like we used to have. What's wrong with them that they need to take the best out of everything? Salad here's vegetables. That's not right.

MUM   You don't have to eat it.

GRANDMA   (PATTING HER PROTECTIVELY) Of course I'll eat it.

MUM	(TO DAD) We're nearly ready.
DAD	I've almost got it.
MUM	Dinner in five?
DAD	I've almost got it.
MUM	(LONG PAUSE) Daniel!
DAD	Alright! I'm coming, I'm coming!
MUM	Go wash your hands and call the boys.
GRANDMA	He's not back yet.
MUM	(FRUSTRATED) That boy!
GRANDMA	He'll be back.
MUM	I don't know what gets into him sometimes.
GRANDMA	He'll be here.
MUM	(TO DAD) Father! I won't ask you again!
DAD	(RISING) Alright, alright. I think it's working anyway.
MUM	Wash your hands.
DAD	You know who invented the projector?
MUM	No! Now go wash your hands!

EXIT DAD.

MUM	(CONT.) You never approved of him, did you?
GRANDMA	He's a good man, in his way.

MUM   He was... I don't understand sometimes. What we do it all for, you know? The family thing. Marriage. I think perhaps we're trying to bottle it, you know what I mean? Something? Just stop it. This moment. This feeling. Just put it all in a bottle and put a cork in it. Because... feelings fade, don't they? Not emotions, but feelings. They fade. And we change. All of us. We don't want what we wanted before. What we have.

It's... Other people, they're just a boat, aren't they. Carrying us down the river. Bobbing along. But they carry us. Other people. Maybe that's the point, do you think? The carrying? Maybe that's what it's all about. Other people: moving us on. Taking us out of where we are. Right now. Maybe we need that. But sooner or later... You can't stay in the boat forever can you? You wouldn't want to! You'd want to get out and stretch your legs and walk and... but then, I guess you'd keep it, the boat. I guess that you would. As a memento. Wouldn't want to get rid of it really; after all the places it took you. You'd want to just hang on to it. And yet we stay there, don't we? You can't get out of the boat! Don't get out of the boat! We just bottle it up and... I suppose it's just comfortable. The bottling. The boat.

GRANDMA   They're good kids.

ENTER MARTY AND DAVID.

MUM   (TO THEM BOTH) Make sure you wash your hands.

MARTY   We're not waiting for him then?

MUM   Wash your hands.

DAVID GOES TO WASH HIS HANDS.

EXIT DAVID.

MARTY   We're not waiting for him?

MUM   He'll be here.

MARTY   This place. I was thinking as I came in. This place is exactly the same as when I was young, you know that? Exactly the same. You'd think, over the years...

MUM   It's home.

MARTY   I guess. You don't think this is all a bit... You know, with everything.

MUM   It's his birthday.

MARTY   Yeah, but...

MUM   He's still your father.

MARTY   Do you remember? That time we were in… I can't remember where. Torquay, I think? We were… it was raining or something and we must have driven down by car because we were waiting there. On the road, next to the beach. And he'd wandered off to… I don't know, but we couldn't leave, could we? We were just there. In the car. For hours. Couldn't go to the beach in the rain, couldn't go home without him. So we just sat there. We sat there and, I remember this, ambulances kept going past. Lots of them. I mean, thinking about it now, we must have been on some route or something but back then, how old was I? Eight? Seven? I really don't remember, but I was there and there were ambulances flashing past and all I kept thinking was…

MUM   You said: "I know he's not a good father, but he's the only one I've got." Which was rude, really.

MARTY   I was a kid.

MUM   You were precocious.

MARTY   Do you remember when I called Grandma a witch? Do you remember that? I was staying there, I think? With her. And she was brushing her hair which was long and white and… well, I'd never seen it down. Not really. She always kept it in a bun.

MUM   Not when she was young.

MARTY   And it reached her waist and I just said: "you look like a witch" and then I thought. That could come out wrong, so I added: "a white witch."

MUM   She told me!

MARTY   You yelled at me so bad!

MUM   It was rude.

MARTY   You've got to be impressed that a ten year old knows the difference between a black witch and a white one.

MUM   You were always precocious.

ENTER DAVID AND DAD.

THE PAIR ARE COMRADES, CHATTING.

DAD   … the entire battle took over eight days, which you never see in any of the movies.

DAVID   Not exactly the point of the movies.

DAD   But what I'm saying is; it took eight days. There were monitors, referees, and if you put your sword down you were treated right. It was like one big game of football really.

DAVID   With really pointy balls.

DAD   You know where football was invented?

DAVID   Rugby?

DAD   Ha! Good one. No. There's these — this is all post-Roman.

MUM   Dinner's ready!

DAD   All over England. These faces, you know, like that one in the movie?

DAVID   Roman Holiday?

DAD   Exactly. Yes. Just like that. They're all over. Every village originally, and what they'd do was, they'd get the whole village together, at the church, which was always placed in the centre of the village — you know why it's called a church, don't you?

MUM   Sit down.

DAD   They'd meet in the middle and they'd have this ball, everyone there, then they'd throw it up in the air and the idea was to move it, by any means possible, from the centre to the other half of the village's 'goal.' Whatever means necessary! Like one big fight.

MUM   David you're over here, by Marty. Marty!

DAVID   Doesn't explain why it's called football though does it.

DAD   Whole game would take an afternoon. Smuggle the ball up your jumper, defend your 'goal'. They still play it some places.

MARTY   You know why it's called the World Series?

DAVID   Cricket?

DAD   The newspaper.

MARTY   He's right. Baseball. It's got nothing to do with how many teams played in it. Nothing at all.

DAD   S'why only Americans.

MARTY   Its original sponsor was 'The World', or something like that, I don't remember. But, anyway, that's why it's called the World Series.

DAD   S' like thinking everyone in the Premiership has to drink lager.

DAVID   Alright, what about Disney…

MUM   That's enough now.

DAD   There is no such thing as a suicidal lemming.

DAVID   Exactly. Drove trucks at them to get them off the cliff.

MARTY   And the sex in The Little Mermaid.

MUM   We are not talking about that here! (THE ROOM QUIETS) Now. Sit down the lot of you or you'll be eating it cold.

MARTY   Where's Kyle?

MUM   He'll have to warm it in the oven.

MARTY   Maybe I should check on him.

MUM   Sit! He'll be back when he's ready. It's your father's birthday.

DAD   He'll be back. Don't worry.

EVERYONE SITS.

MARTY   This looks good.

MUM   It's all your favourites.

MARTY   (TO GRANDMA) Has she been making you help?

GRANDMA   Not making, no.

DAVID   It all looks lovely really.

DAD   Alright. Well. You know, sit, sit.

MARTY   Oh, god. He's going to make a speech isn't he.

DAD   I am. At that. A little speech.

MUM   Before it gets cold.

DAD   It's... Family is important. I don't think there's anything more important, if you know what I mean? My own father... well, he wasn't one such for family, if you know what I mean. But it's important. All of it. There are... there are lots of things we don't know in life but well, we know this, don't we?

MARTY   Can we eat now?

DAD   The name Harrison...

MARTY   Oh god.

DAD   It comes from the time when there weren't names; not last ones. People were called by their profession. Bob Baker: the baker. Jeff Tanner: the tanner.

MARTY   He tells this every year!

DAD   (BEAT) I guess Harrisons must have been collecting benefits then, because our name literally means "Harry's son". So I'm guessing he must have been a bit of an Abraham given how many of us there are out there.

MUM   It's getting cold.

DAD   Anyway. That's family. That's what that is. And It's good to have you all here together. Amen.

GRANDMA   Boy, did I think that was going to go on for a while!

ENTER KYLE AND SARAH.

KYLE ENTERS PULLING A WARY SARAH BEHIND HIM.

KYLE   You got an extra space?

MIX   Kyle! / There you are! / Where've you been?

MARTY RISES AND MOVES AROUND TO KYLE.

KYLE   I found this one wandering the streets looking for a birthday party.

MARTY SUDDENLY AND SURPRISINGLY HUGS HIM.

KYLE   (CONT.) Hey.

MARTY   I'm sorry, little brother. I'm sorry.

KYLE SMILES AND PUSHES HIM BACK. HIS DEMEANOUR IS MUCH CALMER, MUCH MORE COMFORTABLE WITH HIMSELF.

MUM PULLS ANOTHER CHAIR UP TO THE TABLE.

KYLE   You've got nothing to be sorry about. Don't worry.

MUM   (TO SARAH) You sit here. Next to Kyle.

SARAH   I didn't mean to intrude.

MUM   There's plenty of food.

DAD   You're family!

KYLE   (SITTING) You're eating already?

MARTY   It's really good.

KYLE	Did anyone make the toast?
MARTY	Dad just did that name thing.
KYLE	Oh well, glad we missed that!
SARAH	(TO EVERYONE) Thank you.

KYLE   (STANDING) Alright. I've got something to say.

MARTY	Kyle!

KYLE   It'll only take a second. (EVERYONE SETTLES DOWN) This is family. We may not like it. I don't even think we want it really. But those of us here, now, this is who we are. Other people... there are always other people. People who we, you know, maybe even love, people who we maybe... maybe more than the people at this table. And... maybe we've hated people here as well. Doesn't matter. Marty, Emily, Sarah, David. These are family. We are family, and all the wishing in the world isn't going to change that. We are where we belong, and no one made us that way except ourselves. Sooner we come to accept that, the better.

DURING THE SPEECH, EMILY ENTERS, SHAKING SNOW OFF HER COAT. SHE SIGNALS TO THE OTHERS TO BE QUIET AND MOVES UP BEHIND KYLE, TAKING IN THE ROOM WITH SOME AMAZEMENT AS SHE DOES SO.

ONLY MARTY DOESN'T REALLY RESPOND TO HER ARRIVAL.

AS HE FINISHES, SHE PUTS HER HANDS OVER KYLE'S EYES.

EMILY	Guess who?
KYLE	(TURNING) Sis!

EMILY   (HUGGING HIM) Hey big brother. (TO SARAH) Hey cous'.

DAD	Got a hug for your old man.
EMILY	(HUGGING HIM) Hey dad.
MUM	You have things?
DAD	What's with the snow?
EMILY	It's snowing.
DAD	Bollocks!
MUM	Daniel!

EMILY   I left them in the car. Could do with a hand anyway. (TO MARTY) Hey.

MARTY   Hey sis.

EMILY   Yeah, well. I tell you. This place. It's, I tell you, nothing's changed at all!

DAD   You're home now.

EMILY   Give me a hand with my things?

DAD   What you driving?

MUM, DAD, DAVID, AND EMILY HEAD OUT THE FRONT DOOR.

EMILY   Can you believe the snow? Hey, David.

DAVID   I'll give you a hand.

EXIT MUM, DAD, DAVID, AND EMILY.

KYLE TAKES SARAH BY THE HAND AND LEADS HER UPSTAIRS.

KYLE   Come on. I'll show you where you'll sleep.

GRANDMA MOVES TO THE COUCH AND TURNS ON THE PROJECTOR. MARTY STAYS AT THE TABLE PLAYING WITH HIS KNIFE, DESPONDENT.

EXIT KYLE AND SARAH.

GRANDMA   Marty! Come over here. (PAUSE) There's something you need to see.

MARTY   I don't think I'm in the mood for more slides, tell you the truth.

GRANDMA   All the same.

MARTY   (GOING TO THE COUCH) I'm sorry. I never actually... who are you exactly?

GRANDMA   I'm surprised you don't recognize me.

MARTY   Do we know each other?

GRANDMA   You were always the one who noticed things. You ready?

MARTY   You, look a little like my mother. From photographs. When she was younger.

GRANDMA   She looks like me.

MARTY   Are you, I'm sorry, are you family or something?

GRANDMA   I'm your grandmother. Play the slide.

_____**SLIDE**_____ EMILY AS A CHILD IS HUGGING DAVID.

GRANDMA   Not that one. That one's for Emily.

MARTY HITS THE SLIDE.

_____**SLIDE**_____ THE CAR CRASH.

MARTY   I've seen that one.

GRANDMA   Know what it is?

_____**SLIDE**_____ AGAIN. CLOSER.

MARTY   It's...

_____**SLIDE**_____ AGAIN. DIFFERENT ANGLE.

GRANDMA   She had to go home. To her family. And that hurts. I know it does. We're not all family. Not all of us. These are... they're not always apparent. The ties. She had to go home.

_____**SLIDE**_____ AGAIN. DIFFERENT ANGLE.

MARTY   I had a car like that.

_____ **SLIDE** _____ CLOSE UP OF THE DRIVER, MARTY. CLEARLY DEAD BUT NOT CLEARLY MARTY.

MARTY   We were driving from….

_____ **SLIDE** _____ CLOSE UP OF JOSIE IN THE PASSENGER SEAT, ALSO DEAD.

MARTY   And you're really my grandmother?

GRANDMA   And you nearly hit on me. (SHE SMILES) Don't worry about it. Good looking guy like you… (PAUSE) I'll give you some time.

SHE KISSES HIM LIGHTLY ON THE FOREHEAD AND EXITS. MARTY BARELY NOTICES.

_____ **SLIDE** _____ THE CAR CRASH, AMBULANCES ARRIVING.

_____ **SLIDE** _____ THE HOSPITAL. THEY'RE PREPARING TO CRACK JOSIE'S CHEST.

_____ **SLIDE** _____ CLOSE UP OF MARTY AND JOSIE, EMBRACING AS THOUGH FOR A FAMILY ALBUM.

MARTY BURIES HIS FACE IN HIS HANDS AND CRIES.

WE HEAR THE SOUNDS OF THE FAMILY NEARBY OUTSIDE THE DOOR, AND OTHER VOICES UPSTAIRS FROM KYLE AND SARAH. THE FAMILY ARE COMING BACK. WE HEAR FOOTSTEPS ON THE STAIRS.

MARTY WIPES HIS EYES AND TURNS OFF THE PROJECTOR AS HE RISES.

THE DOOR OPENS. THE FAMILY ENTERS. A CACOPHONY OF NOISE. BARNEY THE FAMILY DOG, ALIVE ONCE MORE, RUNS ONSTAGE.

ENTER MUM, DAD, DAVID, EMILY, SARAH AND KYLE.

BLACKOUT.

END OF ACT 4.

CURTAINS.

THOMAS ALEXANDER

Murder Me Gently

Also by

DIRECT

LIGHT

Thomas Alexander

THOMAS ALEXANDER

THE VISITOR

BY

THOMAS ALEXANDER

THE VISITOR

WHEN THE LOVER OF A FAMOUS WRITER GOES MISSING IN A WAR RAVAGED COUNTRY HE BRIBES HIS WAY INTO A JAIL TO QUESTION HER HUSBAND, A MISSIONARY, WHO IS BEING TORTURED AS A TRAINING EXERCISE BY HIS CAPTORS.

ALONE IN THE CELL, THE TWO START A DIALOGUE ABOUT THE NATURE OF BELIEF.

BELIEF IN GOD, LOVE, AND POLITICS.

MURDER ME GENTLY

By

THOMAS ALEXANDER

*"ONE MAN... ONE WOMAN...
AND THE QUEST FOR JUSTICE
IN AN UNJUST WORLD"*

MODERN DAY RUSSIA
THROUGH THE MEDIUM OF
FILM NOIR

BLENDING REAL LIFE EVENTS WITH COMEDY AND INTRIGUE, *MURDER ME GENTLY*'S UNIQUE PERSPECTIVE ON THE WORLD OF RUSSIAN POLITICS AS SEEN THROUGH THE LENS OF FLIM NOIR, SPANS THE ASSASINATION OF INTERNATIONALLY RENOWNED JOURNALISTS, PUTIN'S REACH FOR THE RETURN OF SOVIET SATELITE STATES, AND THE INFLITRATION OF GOVERNMENT BY OLIGARCHS AND CRIMINALS.

PROVIDING A DAMMING INDICTMENT OF THE WEST'S INABILITY TO HALT MOSCOW'S POLICY OF EXPANSIONISM *MURDER ME GENTLY* LENDS A THEATRICAL EXPOSE TO THE VERY REAL WORLD OF CORRUPTION AND GREED IN INTERNATIONAL POLITICS TODAY.

A CONMAN, A DISGRACED INTERPOL AGENT, A MAFIA BOSS, A CIA SPOOK, AND THE SECRET TO THE FUTURE ALL UNITE IN AN UNLIKELY ALLIANCE IN A LOVE AFFAIR THAT WILL DEFINE THE FATE OF THE WORLD IN THOMAS ALEXANDER'S

... MURDER ME ... GENTLY!

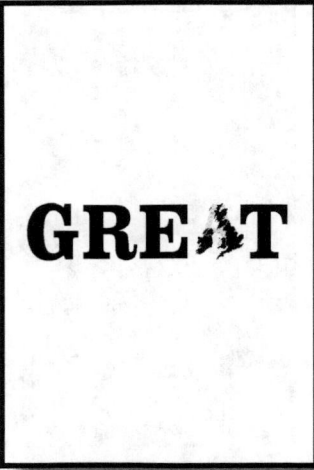

GREAT

BY

THOMAS ALEXANDER

A REMOTE ROOM IN THE THROES OF WINTER.

THE ONCE GREAT MAN LIVES ALONE NOW WITH HIS SON,

AN OLD FRIEND HAS COME TO VISIT. HE HAS CLIMBED UP FROM THE VILLAGE IN ORDER TO OFFER THE OLD MAN ONE LAST CHANCE TO ESCAPE THE ENCROACHING WINTER THAT IS ABOUT TO TAKE HIM, STIRRING UP MEMORIES OF BETTER TIMES AND THE WARMTH OF SUMMER.

BEGAT

BY

THOMAS ALEXANDER

IN A COUNTRY, AFTER THE WAR, A JUDGE THROWS A DINNER PARTY, SEEKING SUPPORT AGAINST A POWERFUL MINISTER WHO HAS RAPED AND KILLED A SERVANT GIRL.

BUT THE JUDGE HIMSELF IS THE TARGET TONIGHT, AND THE SHADOW OF THE WAR HE SO DESPERATELY WANTS TO LEAVE BEHIND THREATENS TO ENGULF HIS FAMILY AS A YOUNG WOMAN SEEKS REVENGE FOR THE SINS OF HIS PAST.

HAPPINESS

BY

THOMAS ALEXANDER

ON A REMOTE HEADLAND IN NORTH
WALES A MAN AND HIS PARAPLEGIC
SON DREAM OF LIFE BEYOND THE
CONFINES OF THEIR FOUR WALLS.

BUT WHEN A WOMAN OFFERS THEM
THE ESCAPE THEY SO CRAVE THEY
FIND THEY ARE BOUND BY MORE
THEN THEIR DREAMS.

THE JEALOUSY OF A BORED
POLICEMAN AND THE KINDNESS OF
A MAIL ORDER BRIDE SET THEM ON A
PATH OF HOPE AND DESTRUCTION.

THE LAST CHRISTMAS

THE LAST CHRISTMAS

BY

THOMAS ALEXANDER

IT'S NEWS!

WHEN AN EMBATTLED NEWSROOM RECEIVES A POTENTIALLY EARTH SHATTERING STORY MINUTES BEFORE AIR ON CHRISTMAS DAY THE CAREFUL EQUILIBRIUM OF THE TEAM IS SHATTERED AND OLD DIVIDING LINES COME TO THE FORE, TURNING CO-WORKER AGAINST CO-WORKER.

SET IN REAL TIME AND INCORPORATING ACTUAL AND INTERCHANGEABLE NEWS EVENTS THE LAST CHRISTMAS PITS SOCIAL POLITICS AGAINST JOURNALISTIC INTEGRITY IN A BATTLE OF THE ETHICS.

GOD

By

Thomas Alexander

When the named partner of a small law firm dies, leaving large debt, the remaining misfits of the firm are forced to take on just about any client available, including a litigious soccer-mom who would like to sue God for the death of her husband, hit by a lightning bolt on the 15th hole of a municipal golf course.

The Trial becomes complicated, however, when an indigent with no background and a canny knack of knowing everyone's background enters the courtroom claiming to be God.

Batting back and fore between the courtroom and the personal lives of the lawyers, God is a fast paced courtroom drama/comedy that uses original staging and non-linear storytelling to provide a lighthearted, but complex social drama.

The Family

By

Thomas Alexander

Today, for the first time in longer than anyone can remember, the family are gathering. They are gathering to celebrate the engagement of the maternal niece, they are gathering to celebrate the last birthday of the patriarch, they are gathering to welcome home the prodigal son and his beautiful girlfriend, and they are going to celebrate all this with a slideshow.

Candid photographs. Photographs of things no one thought anyone else knew about. Photograph taken when no one else was there.

It's all coming out today. In black and white for everyone to see. The remnants of child abuse, infidelity, loss, destruction, and missed birthday parties. It's all coming out. It's going to be a long night. Possibly forever.

THE RECRUITMENT OFFICER

BY

THOMAS ALEXANDER

TOM, A CHARMING YANKEE RECRUITER, COMES TO AN UNSPECIFIED ENGLISH TOWN AND FALLS IN LOVE WITH THE CONFERENCE CENTRE MANAGER, JULIA.

BUT WHAT EXACTLY IS HE RECRUITING FOR? WHY DOES EVERYONE WHO JOINS NEVER COME BACK AND WHAT IS ON THE OTHER SIDE OF THE DOOR

WHERE DO THE RECRUITS GO AFTER SIGNING UP?

AN EXISTENTIAL LOVE STORY THAT ASKS QUESTIONS OF WHO WE ARE, WHAT WE WANT FROM LIFE, AND WHETHER WE'RE GETTING IT, THE RECRUITMENT OFFICER IS A REMODELLING OF THE 1706 PLAY BY GEORGE FARQUHAR, *THE RECRUITING OFFICER.*

WRITER'S BLOCK

BY

THOMAS ALEXANDER

PAUL BLOCK WAS ONCE A PROLIFIC WRITER. A RECIPIENT OF BOTH THE PEN AND FAULKNER AWARDS AND THE AUTHOR OF OVER TEN DIFFERENT NOVELS, HE WAS ONCE CONSIDERED THE UK'S MOST UP AND COMING WRITER UNTIL, AT THE AGE OF FORTY, HE SUFFERED A NERVOUS BREAKDOWN.

TEN YEARS LATER THE WORLD HAS FORGOTTEN PAUL BLOCK. HOLED UP IN HIS STUDY HE HAS BEEN WORKING ON THE SAME FIRST PAGE OF HIS NEW NOVEL FOR NEARLY FIVE YEARS, KEPT COMPANY BY ONLY HIS MAID, A FOUL MOUTHED IRISH HIT-MAN, A VETERAN OF THE BATTLE OF GETTYSBURG AND A NINETEEN FORTIES FEMME FATALE.

TODAY, ALL THAT'S GOING TO CHANGE. PAUL HAS A BUSY DAY AHEAD OF HIM. FIRST HE'S GOING TO KILL A PERSISTENT AND CHARMLESS YOUNG REPORTER WHO WANTS TO DO A PIECE ON 'WRITER'S BLOCK' AND THEN HE'S GOING TO HAVE A RARE VISIT FROM HIS SON WHO'S BRINGING HIM BAD NEWS AND A NEW COUCH.

WITH A MISSING BODY AND A SON WHO HATES HIM, PAUL MUST FINALLY RID HIMSELF OF HIS PROTAGONISTS IF HE'S EVER GOING TO STAY OUT OF JAIL, AND FINISH THAT FIRST PAGE.

THOMAS

Japan, 1945 – A Family At War

When a wandering priest escaping a troubled past is taken in by a prominent family, a quiet city in northern Japan is forced to confront the dark shadows of war seeping into their lives in ways they could never have anticipated.

With its townsmen scattered throughout the farthest ends of a desperate empire in a final defence against the encroaching West, the idyllic northern city of Morioka, far removed from the harsh realities of the front, is largely left to itself.

THOMAS ALEXANDER

But when a prominent doctor is conscripted and sent to Manila, his sister is left as head of the household and must deal with a young priest living at the bottom of their garden with a large collection of maps and strange knowledge of English.

A Scattering of Orphans

As the cold hand of war approaches, each person must choose their own destiny and place in the new world.

THE OTHER SIDE

ALEXANDER

Commemorating the 70th Anniversary of the end of WW2! A trilogy spanning the length of the war from the viewpoint of an ordinary Japanese family.

Thomas Alexander

The Disingenuous Martyr

omas Alexander

Beyond The Noonday Sun

Offering a unique perspective through the eyes of a rural Japanese family into the impact of history's bloodiest war to date, *A Scattering of Orphans* is one family's attempt to make sense of a changing world amidst the desolation of war, both home and abroad.

DIRECT AGENT

OF THE SUN

THOMAS ALEXANDER

THE FAMILY

www.ingramcontent.com/pod-product-compliance
Lightning Source LLC
La Vergne TN
LVHW052033080426
835513LV00018B/2298